D1555173

Qatar

WORLD BIBLIOGRAPHICAL SERIES

General Editors:
Robert L. Collison (Editor-in-chief)
Sheila R. Herstein
Louis J. Reith
Hans H. Wellisch

VOLUMES IN THE SERIES

1 *Yugoslavia*, John J. Horton
2 *Lebanon*, Shereen Khairallah
3 *Lesotho*, Shelagh M. Willet and David Ambrose
4 *Rhodesia/Zimbabwe*, Oliver B. Pollack and Karen Pollack
5 *Saudi Arabia*, Frank A. Clements
6 *USSR*, Anthony Thompson
7 *South Africa*, Reuben Musiker
8 *Malawi*, Robert B. Boeder
9 *Guatemala*, Woodman B. Franklin
11 *Uganda*, Robert L. Collison
12 *Malaysia*, Lim Huck Tee and Wong Sook Jean
13 *France*, Frances Chambers
14 *Panama*, Eleanor Langstaff
15 *Hungary*, Thomas Kabdebo
16 *USA*, Sheila R. Herstein and Naomi Robbins
17 *Greece*, Richard Clogg and Mary Jo Clogg
18 *New Zealand*, R. F. Grover
19 *Algeria*, Richard I. Lawless
21 *Belize*, Ralph Lee Woodward, Jr.
23 *Luxembourg*, Carlo Hury and Jul Christophory
24 *Swaziland*, Balam Nyeko
25 *Kenya*, Robert L. Collison
26 *India*, Brijen Gupta and Datta Kharbas
27 *Turkey*, Meral Güçlü
28 *Cyprus*, P. M. Kitromilides and M. Evriviades
29 *Oman*, Frank A. Clements
30 *Italy*, Emiliana P. Noether
31 *Finland*, J. E. O. Screen
32 *Poland*, Richard C. Lewanski
33 *Tunisia*, Richard I. Lawless, Allan M. Findlay and Anne M. Findlay
34 *Scotland*, Eric G. Grant
35 *China*, Peter Cheng

VOLUME 36

Qatar

P.T.H. Unwin
Compiler

CLIO PRESS

OXFORD, ENGLAND · SANTA BARBARA, CALIFORNIA

British Library Cataloguing in Publication Data

Unwin, P. T. H.
Qatar. – (World bibliographical series; 36)
1. Qatar – Bibliography
I. Title II. Series
016.953.63 Z3028.Q3

ISBN 0-903450-66-6

Clio Press Ltd.,
Woodside House, Hinksey Hill,
Oxford OX1 5BE, England.
Providing the services of the European
Bibliographical Centre and the American
Bibliographical Center

American Bibliographical Center-Clio Press,
Riviera Campus, 2040 Alameda Padre Serra,
Santa Barbara, Ca. 93103, U.S.A.

Designed by Bernard Crossland
Computer typeset by Peter Peregrinus Ltd.
Printed in Great Britain
by the Camelot Press, Southampton

THE WORLD BIBLIOGRAPHICAL SERIES

This series will eventually cover every country in the world, each in a separate volume comprising annotated entries on works dealing with its history, geography, economy and politics; and with its people, their culture, customs, religion and social organization. Attention will also be paid to current living conditions — housing, education, newspapers, clothing, etc. — that are all too often ignored in standard bibliographies; and to those particular aspects relevant to individual countries. Each volume seeks to achieve, by use of careful selectivity and critical assessment of the literature, an expression of the country and an appreciation of its nature and national aspirations, to guide the reader towards an understanding of its importance. The keynote of the series is to provide, in a uniform format, an interpretation of each country that will express its culture, its place in the world, and the qualities and background that make it unique.

SERIES EDITORS

Robert L. Collison (Editor-in-chief) is Professor Emeritus, Library and Information Studies, University of California, Los Angeles, and is currently the President of the Society of Indexers. Following the war, he served as Reference Librarian for the City of Westminster and later became Librarian to the BBC. During his fifty years as a professional librarian in England and the USA, he has written more than twenty works on bibliography, librarianship, indexing and related subjects.

Sheila R. Herstein is Reference Librarian and Library Instruction Coordinator at the City College of the City University of New York. She has extensive bibliographic experience and recently described her innovations in the field of bibliographic instruction in 'Team teaching and bibliographic instruction', *The Bookmark*, Autumn 1979. In addition, Doctor Herstein co-authored a basic annotated bibliography in history for Funk & Wagnalls *New encyclopedia*, and for several years reviewed books for *Library Journal*.

Louis J. Reith is librarian with the Franciscan Institute, St. Bonaventure University, New York. He received his PhD from Stanford University, California, and later studied at Eberhard-Karls-Universität, Tübingen. In addition to his activities as a librarian, Dr. Reith is a specialist on 16th century German history and the Reformation and has published many articles and papers in both German and English. He was also editor of the *American Society for Reformation Research Newsletter*.

Hans H. Wellisch is Associate Professor at the College of Library and Information Services, University of Maryland, and a member of the American Society of Indexers and the International Federation for Documentation. He is the author of numerous articles and several books on indexing and abstracting, and has most recently published *Indexing and abstracting: an international bibliography*. He also contributes frequently to *Journal of the American Society for Information Science, Library Quarterly*, and *The Indexer*.

Contents

Contents

Preface

Although the British were not the first European power to involve themselves in the Gulf they were by far the most significant. As a result the majority of non-Arabic works on Qatar are written in English. A number of French, Danish and German articles have nevertheless been included in this bibliography, since they provide interesting comments on the state, and avoid the possibility of colonial sentimentality. The Danish archaeological expeditions to Qatar have produced much information on its prehistory, and many of their publications have English summaries.

There are very few books or articles written exclusively on Qatar, but the country is mentioned in many texts on oil in the Middle East and on the British involvement in the Gulf. The large number of publications in these fields necessitates a degree of subjectivity in the choice of those to include in this bibliography. In general only publications that provide important background material or more than a passing reference to Qatar have been included.

Qatar features little in the early European explorations of Arabia, but Palgrave halted there on his journey down the Gulf, and Doha formed the end-point of Thomas's crossing of the Rub al-Khali. Other 19th century writers also mentioned the peninsula, and their works are included in the bibliography. It is significant to note that nearly all European maps prior to the last quarter of the 18th century failed to show its existence.

An extensive range of bibliographical sources has been used in compiling this work, and a number of earlier bibliographies relating to the Arabian peninsula are noted in the final section. The aim has been to provide a wide spectrum of basic texts on all the major aspects of the country. However, certain sections, such as those on languages and dialects, science and technology, literature, the arts, and books, are notably poorly represented. This directly reflects the lack of works published in English on these topics. The number of government publications has been kept to a minimum, but where it has been felt that

Preface

they provide important information unavailable elsewhere they have been listed. Many of these can be obtained from the Information or Cultural Departments of Qatar's embassies. Given the general nature of many works on Qatar several problems are encountered in their classification, but these have hopefully been minimised by the use of comprehensive cross-references and a thorough author, subject and title index.

Transliterations from Arabic also present particular difficulties. The approach used in the annotations has been to follow the method used by the author of the work in question. Thus sheikh and shaikh, Katar and Qatar, will be found in the annotations. Traditionally the region in which Qatar lies has been known as the Persian Gulf, and hence most works refer to it as such, despite the Arab use of the phrase Arabian Gulf. In an attempt to remain impartial the simple word Gulf has been used wherever possible in the present work. The transliteration of tribal names also presents difficulties, due to the confusion between *Al* (family) and *al-* (the). While for purists *Al* might appear to be more correct, the use of *Al-* for tribal names is common in the Gulf. In referring to the royal family of Qatar the Press and Publications Department of the Ministry of Information, Qatar, continues to refer to the family as the Al-Thani, with *Al-*, and to individual members of the family, as for example the emir HH Shaikh Khalifa bin Hamad al-Thani, with *al-*. To minimize confusion the introduction of the present volume therefore follows the same system using *Al-* and *al-*.

Acknowledgements are due to Dick Lawless and the staff of the Middle East Documentation Centre at the University of Durham for their patience in putting up with my many enquiries; the staff of the Oriental Library at the University of Durham; Inger Mitchell (Science Library, University of Durham) for her help in providing many copies of the references through inter-library loan; Mona Barsoum and Nora Alamuddin in the Information Office at the Embassy of Qatar in London; Mohammed al-Kubaisi for sharing with me much of his wide-ranging knowledge of Qatar and for commenting on various aspects of the introduction; and my wife Pam for her help in reading through the final text and for providing valuable criticisms of an earlier draft of the book.

Tim Unwin
London
5 November 1981

x

Introduction

The peninsula of Qatar projects from the northern coastline of Arabia. To the east lies the federation of the United Arab Emirates, and the vast desert expanses of Saudi Arabia are to the south. Offshore to the west are found the islands of Bahrain. In the past Qatar was known as the land that God forgot, and early European impressions of the peninsula were no more flattering: in 1865 Palgrave described Bedaa' (Bida), the main town of Qatar, as the miserable capital of a miserable province, and Sir Rupert Hay in 1954 saw the country as possibly the ugliest stretch of territory that God has created. However, the country has seen dramatic economic change since the discovery of oil there in 1939, and especially during the 1970s, following its independence from Britain in 1971 and the restructuring of oil prices in 1973-74. Today, as a Gulf member of the Organization of Petroleum Exporting Countries (OPEC), even if only a small one producing 1.5 per cent of OPEC's total oil, it lies close to the centre of world attention. Doha, the capital, is a modern city, with facilities and infrastructure as advanced as anywhere in the world.

Qatar is located between 50° 45' and 51° 40' east, and 24° 30' and 26° 10' north. It is 85 kilometres at its widest and 165 kilometres long, and together with its islands it covers a total area of 11,400 square kilometres. Geologically Qatar is composed of Tertiary limestones and dolomites with interbedded clays, marls and shales, which, in places, are covered by Quaternary and Recent superficial deposits. The most extensive formations are the dolomites and chalky limestones of the Upper Dammam of middle Eocene age. The peninsula is essentially a wide anticlinal dome, whose north-south axis is central to the country. This is complicated by the presence of a number of other structures, notably the Dukhan anticline, which is the main oil-bearing structure, the Simsimah dome, and the Sawda Nathil dome. There are numerous coastal *sabkha* deposits, *sabkha* being the Arabic term for saline mud flats, and there are also extensive areas of sand dunes, particularly in the Khawr al-'Udaid region in the south-east. The highest elevation, 103 metres, is found in the south of the peninsula. There are numerous small depressions, especially in the centre and north, in which are found soils of colluvium origin termed *rawdah*. These provide the main source of land for agriculture.

Qatar has a hot climate, which at different times of the year can be dry or very humid. Between November and February temperatures range from between 7°C to 30°C. This is followed by a period up to mid-May when the temperatures rise rapidly, remaining at daily maximum figures of over 42°C until July. During this time strong north-westerly winds are also common. Between August and October the wind decreases, but relative humidity greatly increases. Virtually all of the rainfall occurs in the winter, but even then average figures are normally only in the order of seventy-five millimetres per annum.

The environmental history of the Gulf is complex, and as yet not fully understood, but it is clear that at some stage much of the Gulf was dry land. According to Vita-Finzi, the marine transgression after c.44,000 BP led to a period of about 14,000 years when Qatar was provided with coastal resources suitable for a hunter-gatherer population. A further fall in sea level, reaching its maximum about 15,000 BP, is seen as leading to basin filling through flash flood deposition, and also the creation of *sabkha* deposits.

The majority of archaeological sites investigated lie around the coasts of the peninsula. The first archaeological investigations were undertaken by Danish expeditions between 1956 and 1964, and these have been supplemented by the British expedition which studied the region during the planning of the National Museum in the early 1970s. These have revealed a number of palaeolithic, mesolithic and neolithic prehistoric sites in the country, indicating small encampments, seasonal settlements and flint-working sites occupied at various times between 50,000 and 7,000 years ago. In addition Ubaid pottery has been found in several neolithic sites. This comes from one of the earliest Middle Eastern pottery cultures, dating from the sixth to the fourth millenia BC. Numerous burial mounds have also been identified, particularly in the Ras Abaruk peninsula. Examples of the discoveries made include a mesolithic settlement at Wusail, a large town area dating to the middle of the first millenium BC at Murwab, and a large surface-chipping flint site five kilometres south of Dukhan. Rock carvings have been found at Wakrah and Fuwayrat. The presence of many of the Stone Age sites along the coast suggests that the majority of communities were involved in fishing or trade.

Little is known of Qatar before the 18th century, although Islam was brought to the peninsula in 628 AD by Al-A'la bin Abdullah al-Hadhrahmi, the envoy of the prophet Muhammad. It was the voyage

Introduction

of Vasco da Gama round the Cape of Good Hope in 1498 that led to the opening up of the Gulf to European influence. Bahrain became a Portuguese possession in 1521, following the earlier fall of Muscat and Hormuz. However, two main forces prevented complete Portuguese domination of the Gulf in the remainder of the 16th century. On the one hand the Ottomans were vying for control of the region, although they failed to take Hormuz from the Portuguese, and on the other hand the emergence of Safavid power in Persia countered Portuguese influence. The Portuguese had planned, and for a time succeeded in creating, a hegemony of trade from the East to Europe by blocking the traditional routes through the Gulf, the Red Sea and the Straits of Malacca, and forcing trade to be carried in Portuguese boats. However, by 1600, and the establishment of the English East India Company, Portuguese power had begun to wane. From then until the 20th century the history of the Gulf became increasingly connected with British interests in India. Nevertheless, for a century before Britain's control of the Gulf, another European power, namely Holland, achieved supremacy in the region. For parts of the 18th century the English East India Company maintained factories at Bushire and Basra, but with the collapse of Safavid power in the middle of the century there was anarchy in Persia. Throughout this period Qatar can be assumed to have played a minor role, having few physical assets to favour it.

Around 1760 members of the Al-Khalifa section of the Utub tribe from Kuwait migrated to Zubarah in the north-west of Qatar. At this date there were perhaps only three fishing villages on the peninsula, all in the east, namely Huwaylah, Fuwayrat, and al-Bida later known as Doha. The main tribes on the peninsula were then probably the Al-Musallam, the Sudan, the Maadhid, and the Al-bin-Ali. Zubarah soon grew into an important trading centre, with its fortune based largely on pearling and fishing. Bahrain at this time was occupied by Persians, and as Zubarah grew in importance conflict emerged between the two countries. After several unsuccessful skirmishes the Utub eventually captured Bahrain in 1783, when most of the Al-Khalifa left Qatar and settled in the newly conquered island. Bahrain soon eclipsed Zubarah in importance, possibly because of the better quality of the pearls found surrounding the islands, and Qatar's role declined. The Al-Khalifa, now at Bahrain, claimed suzerainty over Qatar, but the Jalahimah, another section of the Utub, who had returned to Zubarah after the invasion of Bahrain, rejected this and sought their independence forming a new settlement north of Zubarah at Khawr Hassan.

At this time Qatar became involved in the mainstream of Arabian affairs as the Wahhabi movement, a puritanical Islamic movement

Introduction

founded by Muhammad bin Abd al-Wahhab and initially led by the House of Saud, spread outwards from Nejd. The Wahhabis made their first incursions into Qatar in 1787 and 1788, and the leader of the Jalahimah, Rahmah bin Jabir, formed an alliance with them in order to overthrow the Al-Khalifa. At this stage three other external powers emerged on the scene. The Ottomans were afraid of the rising Wahhabi power in Arabia and thus launched an attack on the Hijaz. At the same time Sayyid Said bin Sultan, ruler of Muscat and Oman, attacked the Wahhabis in Qatar, and destroyed Zubarah. These two factors led to the evacuation of the Wahhabis from Qatar. The third power to appear was Britain, whose ships were being molested by the Qawasim, whose main stronghold was well east of Qatar at Ras al-Khaimah. However, Bahrain was being used by the Qawasim as a safe harbour, and in order not to provoke the anger of the British navy the ruler of Bahrain signed a peace treaty with Britain. In 1819 the British had destroyed Ras al-Khaimah, and in 1820 signed the General Treaty of Peace with the Qawasim. The treaty signed between Britain and Bahrain provided that the inhabitants of Bahrain would abstain from piracy and would become a party to the General Treaty of Peace signed with the Qawasim. Since the rulers of Bahrain laid claim to Qatar it was assumed that it too was a party to the agreements.

In 1861 Bahrain signed a further agreement with Britain agreeing to the cessation of all maritime warfare in exchange for British protection from attacks by sea. Qatar, although not mentioned specifically, was probably referred to in this agreement as being within Bahrain's dependencies. At this time the authority of Bahrain in Qatar was administered from Doha by a *wali*, or deputy, who was a member of the Al-Khalifa. However, after a period of unrest, for which many causes have been suggested, the *wali* was forced by the inhabitants to leave Doha in 1867. Muhammad bin Khalifa of Bahrain then formed an alliance with Shaikh Zayid bin Khalifa of Abu Dhabi, and sacked the towns of Wakrah and Doha in October 1867. The people of Qatar retaliated, but although the ensuing battle led to many casualties, there was no clear victory. In 1868 the British Political Resident in the Gulf, Colonel Lewis Pelly, went to Bahrain and exacted from the ruler a fine for this violation of the 1861 agreement. He then signed an agreement at Wakrah with Shaikh Muhammad bin Thani of Doha to the effect that the latter would also desist from maritime warfare. The Al-Thani had moved to Doha from Fuwayrat soon after 1847, and this notification of their importance by the British strengthened the position of the Al-Thani in Qatar. They nevertheless still had to pay annual tribute to the Al-Khalifa of Bahrain.

Introduction

In 1871 Qasim bin Muhammad al-Thani, the shaikh's son, accepted the Turks into Doha, against his father's wishes, and thus an Ottoman presence was introduced to Qatar. As a result no further tribute was paid to Bahrain, although later the Ottomans demanded an even greater payment as tribute. In 1878 Qasim sacked Zubarah to punish the inhabitants, members of the Naim tribe, for piracy. Although Bahrain laid claim to Zubarah the British Political Resident refused Shaikh Isa of Bahrain permission to help the Naim. In 1879 Qasim was made governor of Doha by the Ottomans, but by the end of the century he had resisted Turkish attempts to impose their own administration in Qatar. Finally, in the Anglo-Turkish Convention of 19 July 1913 the Ottoman Empire renounced all rights to Qatar, and although the shaikh of Bahrain still tried to claim tribute from Qatar according to the 1868 treaty the British refused to permit this.

On 3 November 1916 Abdallah bin Qasim al-Thani, who had succeeded his father as shaikh on the latter's death, formally signed an agreement with Britain which brought Qatar into the trucial system; the other shaikhs having signed similar agreements in 1892. In this agreement Qatar agreed to abstain from piracy, the slave trade and maritime warfare, and to abide by the exclusive agreements concerning relations with foreign powers and the non-alienation of territory. Britain was thus to be consulted before Qatar had any relations with foreign powers. In exchange Britain agreed to protect Qatar from agression by sea and by land.

Prior to the 20th century Qatar's economy had been based on pearling, fishing and trade. The number of villages along the coast had increased, each sited close to a major well, but there was still negligible settled agriculture in the peninsula. By 1900 the main tribes inhabiting the villages on the coast were the Salatah, the Sudan, the Mahandah, the Al-bu-Kuwarah, the Hamaydat, the Al-bu-Aynayu, the Al-bin-Ali and the Huwalah. In addition several nomadic bedouin tribes were known to migrate to Qatar with their herds. The most important of these were the Murrah, the Ajman, the Naim and the Manasir.

Until the 1930s the British involvement in Qatar was minimal, but with the discovery of oil in the Gulf the political and economic situation changed dramatically. It was the discovery of oil above any other single factor that led to the increased involvement of external powers in the affairs of Qatar and also the need for firmly delimitated boundaries. Previously there had been no absolute national boundaries in Arabia, and the only territorial divisions were the *dira* (pasture districts) of the tribes.

During the 1930s the Japanese began producing cultured pearls, and this hit hard at the local pearling economies of the Gulf, and in particular Qatar. Oil had been discovered in Bahrain in 1932, and this together with the pearl recession led to the migration of many people from Qatar to Bahrain and Saudi Arabia in search of work and wealth. The discoveries of oil set in motion a period of intense rivalry between British and American companies who were attempting to gain other oil concessions in the region. The Americans, in general, proved to be more successful in their bargaining, and Socal (Californian Standard Oil Company) quickly obtained a concession from Ibn Saud in Saudi Arabia. If Britain had not possessed the exclusive agreements with the Gulf emirates it seems highly likely that the whole of Arabia would have become an American oil province. As it was, Shaikh Abdallah of Qatar signed an oil concession with the Anglo-Persian Oil Company (APOC) for seventy-five years on 17 May 1935, giving them exclusive rights to the production, transportation, refining and marketing of petroleum and natural gases. If oil was discovered the payments to the ruler were to be three rupees per ton. Immediately following this the concession was transferred to Petroleum Development (Qatar) Ltd., and by October 1939 the first oil discovery was made in the Dukhan field. The Second World War prevented further exploration and development, and it was not until 1949 that the first oil was exported from the Umm Said terminal on the east coast.

In 1935, when the oil concession was signed, Qatar's southern border with Saudi Arabia had not been defined. However, as soon as this previously barren land achieved economic significance it became of great importance to clearly delimit the boundaries. After a period of inactivity during the Second World War the boundary dispute with Saudi Arabia reared its head during the 1950s, and was not finally settled until 1965 when the shaikh of Qatar renounced his claim to Khawr al-'Udaid in favour of the Saudis. A further complication was the claim by Bahrain on the Hawar islands, and the old Al-Khalifa claim on Zubarah. In 1936 Bahrain claimed the Hawar islands, which lie only a very short distance off the west coast of Qatar, by posting there a military garrison. This led to a complaint by Shaikh Abdallah to the British Political Resident, who replied that Bahrain possessed a *prima facie* claim through the presence of its garrison. After further evidence had been presented to the British Political Resident he finally awarded the islands surprisingly to Bahrain in 1939, much to the chagrin of Qatar. Likewise during 1937 the Naim in the north-west rose in revolt with the support of Shaikh Hamad bin Isa of Bahrain, but they were severely defeated by Shaikh Abdallah. After 1945 further disputes concerning Zubarah flared, but eventually these faded and the Zubarah area became fully integrated into Qatar. The Hawar dispute, however, still remains unsettled in 1981.

Introduction

By 1944 Shaikh Abdallah had handed over most of the duties of ruler to his second son and heir Hamad. However, by the time Abdallah abdicated in 1949 because of old age Hamad had also died, and Abdallah's eldest son Ali became ruler. In 1949 a British Political Agent was also appointed to Qatar, to be aided by two advisors.

It was not until the 1960s, though, that major changes took place in Qatar. Until that time pearling, though suffering from the severe effects of Japanese cultured pearl competition, fishing and trade provided the mainstay of the economy. There is some evidence that Qatar suffered from emigration during the Second World War, but the population level at this time was in the region of 28,000, of which perhaps forty per cent were foreign. During the 1950s a few small farms were, for the first time, established to the north of Doha, deriving their irrigation water from pumped groundwater. This proved to be a major new development, since there was no tradition of oasis agriculture in Qatar.

In 1952 an oil concession covering the entire continental shelf offshore area was acquired by the Shell Company. The rights of this concession were transferred in 1954 to Shell Qatar Ltd. By 1960, before the offshore oil production actually commenced, Qatar's onshore flow had risen from its first 800,000 barrels in 1949 to a level of 60,360,000 barrels per annum. During this period little of the oil revenue appears to have been directed to major national development schemes. In 1943 Shaikh Abdallah had begun to build Qatar's first hospital, and in 1956 the modern education system, based on primary, intermediate and secondary state education, was introduced. However, much of the wealth remained in the hands of the ruling family. The financial régime at the time allowed a quarter of the oil revenue to the ruling shaikh, a quarter for all of the other Al-Thani shaikhs, a quarter for the family's reserve fund, and the remaining quarter for the rest of the population. When these figures are considered the gross imbalance must be slightly redressed by the consideration that the Al-Thanis and their dependents included a relatively high proportion of the native Qataris in the country.

During Shaikh Ali's reign many stories circulated concerning his financial extravagance, and it is clear that he spent much of his time out of the shaikhdom, often hunting in Pakistan or staying at his villa near Geneva. Although he had promised on his succession that his brother Hamad's son, Khalifa, would succeed him, Shaikh Ali abdicated in 1960 on the grounds of ill-health in favour of his own son Ahmad. During the 1960s Khalifa bin Hamad was deputy ruler, and with his cousin Ahmad's frequent absence from Qatar he came to achieve considerable power and influence in the country. In 1963 the first signs of social unrest became apparent. The immediate cause of the so-called

Introduction

strike of 1963 was an incident on 19 April when a young nephew of the ruler opened fire on a group of demonstrators who had blocked his car. Two days later a general strike was called, and a National Unity Front was formed. This made several demands, complaining about the privileges of the ruling family, the need for welfare services, the employment of foreigners, and demanding the creation of a municipal council. By the beginning of May, however, the strike ended accompanied by some unclearly defined promises of reform.

During the 1960s economic change progressed at a relatively slow pace. The Water Department had been established as early as 1954 in recognition of the growing needs for fresh water. The first desalination unit was constructed, and in 1963 the Central Desalination Station was built at Ras Abu Aboud. In the late 1960s the increased demands for water led to a second phase expansion of the plant and daily production capacity reached 20 million gallons. In 1962 the Department of Petroleum Affairs was established to control all of the activities of the oil companies operating in the country. In addition to the onshore Dukhan field the major offshore fields discovered in the 1960s were the Idd al-Shargi (1960), the Maidan Mahzan field (1963), the Bunduq field (1964) and the Bulhanine field (1969). Offshore production begain in 1964, when total annual oil production reached a new peak of 77,640,000 barrels. As a result of the marine boundary agreement made between Qatar and Abu Dhabi on 20 March 1969, the Bunduq field became jointly owned by both countries, and in 1970 a special company, the Bunduq Company Ltd., was formed to appraise and develop it. Despite the increased revenue consequent on the oil exports, only one main industrial project in the non-oil sector was developed in the 1960s. This was the Qatar National Cement Company, established in 1965, with production starting in 1969 at a capacity of 100,000 tonnes per year.

It was during the 1960s that major population immigration and the consequent expansion in the construction industry began. By 1969 the population was approximately 80,000, of which sixty per cent were immigrants. Labour laws were first established in 1962, and by the end of the decade the Departments of Legal Affairs, of Finance, and of Administrative Affairs had been established. Educational facilities had also improved during the 1960s. However, by January 1968, when the Labour government in Britain announced its planned termination of all of its defence commitments east of Suez, the country had few signs of economic security. Construction was the main non-oil industry, and modern roads, harbours, and the airport at Doha had been developed. Irrigated agriculture had expanded fourfold between 1960 and 1970 to a total of 411 farms.

Introduction

1968 saw much activity in the Gulf as the rulers of the emirates attempted, with the help of Britain, to formulate a political structure within which their security and development could be achieved after Britain's withdrawal. Given the traditional tribal conflicts, different degrees of economic development, the varying aspirations of the shaikhs, and the vastly different oil resources, this was to prove to be a complex procedure. The first serious consideration was to unite all of the nine Gulf emirates which had previously been under British administration, Bahrain, Qatar, Abu Dhabi, Dubai, Sharjah, Ajman, Umm al-Qaiwain, Ras al-Khaimah and Fujairah, into a single union. In February 1968 a summit meeting of the rulers of these states was held in Dubai, and the government of Qatar proposed that a federation of Arab emirates should be established with both a higher council, consisting of the rulers, and a federal council for administration. A declaration of unity was made, and in July 1968 Khalifa bin Hamad of Qatar was elected chairman of the Temporary Federal Council. However, in May 1969 the nine rulers failed to reach any major agreements at a meeting in Doha. The fundamental source of conflict lay between Bahrain and Qatar, based on the traditional rivalry between the Al-Khalifa and the Al-Thani. Bahrain had the largest population and highest degree of infrastructural development, and thus wished to play a leading role in the proposed federation. Qatar could not agree to this. At the beginning of 1970 Shaikh Isa bin Hamad stated his determination for individual independence for Bahrain by announcing the formation of his first Cabinet. Although Qatar still paid lip service to the concept of federation, it then announced the enactment of a provisional constitution in April 1970. This declared Qatar to be an independent sovereign Arab state, with Islam as its religion, and the *sharia* as its fundamental law. Partly through pressure from members of his family and the British, Shaikh Ahmad then transferred all of his authority to his cousin Shaikh Khalifa bin Hamad, who became *de facto* ruler.

On 1 January 1970 the first Council of Ministers was sworn into office in Qatar, with seven of the ten members of the Cabinet being members of the ruling Al-Thani family. Finally on 1 September 1971 Shaikh Khalifa bin Hamad al-Thani announced Qatar's intention to terminate its treaties with Britain, and on 3 September Qatar became an independent state with full sovereignty. At the same time it joined the Arab League and the United Nations. Shaikh Ahmad did not return to Qatar during the independence celebrations, and while hunting with his falcons in Iran in the last week of February 1972 he was finally deposed by his cousin Shaikh Khalifa who proclaimed himself ruler.

The Amended Provisional Constitution of 1971 provides that the emir represents both the legislative and executive sections of the

Introduction

government and is assisted by the Council of Ministers and the Advisory Council. The rulership of Qatar is stated to be hereditary in the Al-Thani family, and since independence the head of state has remained Shaikh Khalifa bin Hamad. He is also supreme commander of the armed forces, and in May 1977 he announced the appointment of his eldest son and heir apparent Shaikh Hamad bin Khalifa Al-Thani commander-in-chief of the armed forces and minister of defence. The Council of Ministers is the highest executive body of the state and is appointed by the head of state. Its role is to draft and supervise legislation, to plan development policy, and to control the administration and finance of government, to supervise the civil service, and to uphold foreign relations in accordance with the law. The council consists of fifteen ministers from the following Ministries: Defence, Interior, Foreign Affairs, Finance and Petroleum, Education, Economy and Commerce, Electricity and Water, Industry and Agriculture, Municipal Affairs, Justice, Public Works, Communications and Transport, Public Health, Labour and Social Affairs, and Information.

In accordance with Article 40 of the Amended Provisional Constitution an Advisory Council was established in April 1972 to assist the emir and the Council of Ministers. The Advisory Council now consists of thirty members who are appointed by the emir's decree, and its terms of reference are to discuss and review all aspects of the state's policy and draft legislation, and to request information from the Council of Ministers in order to aid review processes and to submit recommendations. The Advisory Council has created four committees for Legal and Legislative Affairs, Financial and Economic Affairs, Public Services and Utilities, and Domestic and Foreign Affairs and Information.

Since independence the country's economy has seen major changes. Agriculture has expanded, but, although accurate figures are hard to obtain, it seems clear that, due to increased water resource problems and soil salinity, the number of non-producing farms has increased. At the same time, though, the number of producing farms has also increased from 338 in 1975 to 406 in 1979. All agricultural land is vested in the government, and most farm owners participate only indirectly in the farming process, having permanent positions in other sectors, often in government. As a consequence the majority of farms are administered by immigrant managers employing Omani, Palestinian, Iranian and Egyptian labour. The government has established an experimental farm centre, and a comprehensive survey of agriculture in the state has been undertaken in co-operation with the United Nations Development Programme and Food and Agriculture Organization.

Introduction

The development of agriculture and industry has, however, been totally dependent on the expansion of the oil sector. Oil, while being by far the most dominant sector, providing ninety per cent of the state's revenue, has provided the possibility of only limited economic diversity. Qatar became an OPEC member in 1961, being the first non-founder member to join, and in 1972 the Qatar National Petroleum Company was created to supervise oil operations within the country. However, following OPEC's decisions in 1974 to raise the price of oil and to obtain more direct control over the oil industry, the Qatar General Petroleum Corporation (QGPC) was established by Law No. 10 of 4 July 1974. Its aim was to work for the development of the oil industry in all its aspects, including exploration and prospecting for oil and natural gas, and the production, refining, transport, trading, distribution, sale and export of these substances. In December 1974 the government announced that it intended to purchase the remaining forty per cent share in the ownership of Qatar Petroleum Company (QPC) and the Shell Company of Qatar. After long negotiations the state took over the assets and rights of QPC in September 1976, and in February 1977 those of the Shell Company of Qatar. In 1976 the Qatar Petroleum Producing Authority (QPPA) was also established as a wholly owned subsidiary of QGPC to operate the onshore and offshore crude oil production. By 1980, though, the QPPA had become fully merged with the QGPC and ceased to exist as a separate entity. Offshore production has played an increasingly important role, and in 1973 for the first time it exceeded that of the onshore field. In that year onshore production was 91,650,000 barrels and offshore production attained 116,730,000 barrels. Since then production levels have fluctuated with, for example, a total of only 159,480,000 barrels being produced in 1975. The 1979 level was 184,800,000 barrels, of which 54.5 per cent came from the offshore fields, and oil revenue that year reached a figure of Qatari riyals 11,220 million. Early in 1981 the oil production rate was reduced from 500,000 barrels per day to 360,000 barrels per day in the face of the world oil surplus and the realization of the limited extent of Qatar's oil reserves. Future production levels will nevertheless remain uncertain, reflecting both the national conservation interests and also the wider policies of OPEC.

Until recently most natural gas was flared off; in 1976 the average daily onshore production was 272 million cubic feet per day of which 54.3 per cent was flared. However, by 1979 onshore gas production had attained 436 million cubic feet per day, with only 4.6 per cent being flared. In 1975 work began on a natural gas liquids (NGL) plant at Umm Said, and the recent find of a major gas field in the North West

Introduction

Dome, now called the North Field, will provide Qatar with energy for many years to come. Although Qatar's oil reserves are expected to last until 2015, its gas reserves are now conservatively estimated at 70-100 trillion cubic feet, which will last very much longer.

Qatar's main industrial activity has naturally been in the field of oil and gas, despite the government's attempts at diversification. Its first major oil refinery, at Umm Said, was commissioned in 1974 for the National Oil Distribution Company (NODCO), which had been founded in October 1968 for the refining and distribution of oil products within Qatar. This added to the capacity of the earlier very small refinery established in 1953 with a daily production of only 600 barrels. The Umm Said refinery had an initial capacity of 6,200 barrels per day, and it was enlarged in 1977 to provide a total capacity of 11,500 barrels per day. Following the 1973-74 upheaval in the oil industry, the government decided to enlarge its downstream activities and to construct an export-oriented refinery. This is to be on a site adjacent to the NODCO refinery at Umm Said, and production is expected to begin in 1983.

Umm Said, forty kilometres south of Doha, has become the industrial heart of Qatar, and in 1975 a natural gas liquids (NGL) plant was constructed there. This first plant was badly damaged by fire in 1977, but had been reconstructed by the end of 1980, when its daily production was 740 tonnes of propane, 470 tonnes of butane and 310 tonnes of condensate natural gasoline. It can also produce 2.3 million cubic metres per day of ethane-rich gas and 4 million cubic metres per day of methane-rich gas. A second natural gas liquids plant, NGL No. 2, was also commissioned in 1980. This is to cater for the offshore gas production and has the following daily capacities: 230 tonnes of propane, 730 tonnes of butane, 73 tonnes of condensate, 0.9 million cubic metres of ethane-rich gas, and 3 million cubic metres of methane-rich gas.

Gas feedstocks also supply two fertilizer plants. In 1969 the Qatar Fertilizer Company (QAFCO) was incorporated, and since 1975 QGPC has held seventy per cent of its share capital and Norsk Hydro twenty-five per cent. The first plant began production at Umm Said in 1973, being supplied by a 24-inch natural gas pipeline from the Dukhan field eighty kilometres away. Work on a second plant QAFCO II at Umm Said began in 1976, and production at the same levels as the first plant began in 1979.

The final major downstream activity in which Qatar is involved is petrochemicals. The Qatar Petrochemical Company (QAPCO) was established in 1974, and its facilities at Umm Said were commissioned in various phases during 1980 and 1981. At present it consists of an ethylene plant, a LDPE plant, and a power and steam generator complex.

Introduction

The industrial economy is thus clearly strongly, and some would say dangerously, dominated by oil. However, the large resources of gas should ensure that the NGL plants, the fertilizer production, and QAPCO have long-term futures. The government's avowed aims have, though, been for diversification. To this end an agreement was signed with two Japanese companies in 1974 for the construction and operation of a steel plant, to be called Qatar Steel Company Ltd. (QASCO). This plant has also been constructed at Umm Said, and consists of a direct reduction plant, two electric arc furnaces, two continuous casting machines, and a rolling mill. It began commercial production in April 1978, and its power and water requirements are supplied by the Ras Abu Fontas power station. By 1980 its production levels were 420,179 tonnes of sponge iron, 450,449 tonnes of billets, and 430,340 tonnes of reinforcing bars, and the main markets were Saudi Arabia, Kuwait, the UAE, Oman, Bahrain and Iraq. Its major supplier of steel scrap was the USA. In connection with the steel complex a lime kiln has also been constructed at Umm Bab on the west of the peninsula, which produced 17,000 tonnes of lime in 1980.

Other industries in Qatar include crane manufacturing and ship repair work at Umm Said, which has become the industrial centre of the country. The new port facilities there supply both the iron and steel and petrochemical plants. Umm Said has now become a major residential centre, and the population is likely to rise appreciably in the early 1980s. Its fresh water is supplied by the Ras Abu Fontas desalination plant through a 34-kilometre long pipeline.

Although Qatar has no overall development plan, much has clearly been achieved in the industrial sector over the last decade. However, the future of the economy must remain in some doubt due to a number of factors. Firstly, it still remains heavily based on the oil sector; secondly, it is increasingly apparent that the duplication of facilities among Arab countries of the Gulf is leading to overcapacity; thirdly, this development has been manned by a very large immigrant labour force; and fourthly, the water supply situation is becoming critical.

Desalination plants are being expanded, but with present technology these consume large amounts of energy. One positive new development is the planned gas desalination plant at Ras Laffan, which will provide water for agricultural use. Water from this will also be pumped into the aquifer to replace that which has been lost through excessive extraction in the 1970s.

There is evidently a need for some form of agreement on industrial rationalisation in the Gulf, and the Gulf Co-operation Council formed between Bahrain, Kuwait, Oman, Qatar, Saudi Arabia and the UAE in May 1981, although initially concerned with the defence of the region,

Introduction

may provide the basis for future economic co-operation. The generally conservative development policy of Qatar, though, means that the state has suffered fewer of the excesses of economic development found elsewhere in the region.

Qatar's financial policy is controlled by the Ministry of Finance and Petroleum, which indicates the close relationship existing between these two sectors of the economy. In 1966 a Qatar-Dubai currency authority was established for the issue and redemption of currency, but it had no real powers relating to monetary policy or concerning the banking system. Following independence the Qatar Monetary Agency was established in May 1973 to regulate the currency, to protect the value of the riyal, to promote sound banking, and to supervise the bank. As yet the Monetary Agency has had little control over the monetary system, but during 1981 it seems likely that it will at last achieve dominance. Until 1979 the independent banks fixed their interest rates through a gentlemen's agreement, but since then they have been determined by the government. Although the Monetary Agency acts in many ways like a central bank, it is the Qatar National Bank that acts as the government's banker. The other two Qatari banks in the country are the Doha Bank, which was established in 1979, and the Commercial Bank of Qatar, opened in 1975. In 1979 there were ten other foreign banks in Qatar, and these are only permitted to maintain one branch each in the country.

The government has acknowledged the importance of the physical infrastructure of a country in determining the rate of its economic expansion. From the earliest days of independence Qatar has thus spent much of its budget on public works, roads and port improvements, electricity supply, telecommunications, Doha airport, and the Doha sewerage scheme. One indication of this expanded infrastructure is the growth in the number of telephone subscribers from 8,143 in 1971 to 17,700 in 1978. The country's power is supplied by three main power stations, those at Ras Abu Aboud from 1963, Al-Arish from 1975, and Ras Abu Fontas from 1977. The government has also paid much attention to social welfare, and the achievements in the material aspects of this field as presented in the official statistics are impressive.

Education has been at the forefront of government concern, and every citizen has the right to free education. By 1979 there were 122 schools in the country, half of which were for girls. The modern system of primary, intermediary and secondary education was instituted in 1956, when a total of 1,388 boys were educated. Education for girls began in 1957 and since then the numbers of children within the system have risen to 18,531 in 1970 and 33,893 in 1978. In 1973

Introduction

courses were begun for men and women at the Higher Teacher Training Colleges, and these formed the nucleus for the new university. In 1977 the emir issued a law establishing the University of Qatar, divided into four Faculties, those of Education, Science, Humanities and Social Science, and Sharia and Islamic Law. In 1980-81 a fifth Faculty, that of Engineering, was added. There is also a major campaign to abolish illiteracy, and an adult education department whose main aim is to achieve this has been established.

The state provides a free medical service, which is available for both citizens and expatriates. Doha is served by four hospitals, the Rumailah, the Doha Hospital for Contagious Diseases, the Maternity Hospital, and the New Quarantine Hospital. In addition the Hamad General Hospital is being constructed, and when complete it will provide 660 beds. The allocations to public health in the budgets for 1976, 1977 and 1978 were QR 93 million, QR 82 million, and QR 133 million respectively.

There is also a state public housing scheme for Qatari citizens, whereby land is given free to the beneficiaries. In addition an interest-free loan for the actual construction of the housing is available. Prior to 1978, 3,255 government-built houses had been occupied. Social security has been provided for certain categories of citizens since the enactment of the Social Security Law of 1963. The people eligible for this financial assistance must be: unable to earn their living due to illness, injury, or old age; widows who have no breadwinners or who have children; divorcees who have no breadwinners, or who live with relatives who are unable to support them; orphans and children who have no bread-winners; or needy schoolchildren or students on scholarships.

Despite the achievements Qatar has made over the last decade several questions undoubtedly remain as to the future stability of the state. The industrial developments undertaken have been achieved through the exploitation of limited petroleum resources and through the labour of thousands of immigrants. While gas reserves, expected to last well over a century, will enable Qatar's economic base to be sustained, approximately seventy per cent of the population are not citizens. This imbalance of the social structure may well be a source of unrest and political instability during the 1980s. At a time when the Gulf is in ferment, partly under pressure from the external powers of the West and the Soviet Union, the path to future security and prosperity lies fraught with dangers.

The Country and Its People

1 **The Middle East: a handbook.**
Edited by Michael Adams. London: Anthony Blond, 1971.
633p. 17 maps.
An introduction to the Middle East divided into six parts: general background,
the countries of the Middle East, political affairs, economic affairs, social patterns, and the arts and mass media. It includes some basic information and
statistics on Qatar in the 1960s.

2 **Historical and cultural dictionary of the Sultanate of Oman and
the emirates of eastern Arabia.**
John Duke Anthony, with contributions and assistance from
John Peterson, Donald Sean Abelson. Metuchen, New Jersey:
Scarecrow Press, 1976. 136p. bibliog. (Historical and Cultural
Dictionaries of Asia, no. 9).
This useful book gives details of the place- and personal-names of Qatar, includ-
ing information on the Al-Thani ruling family.

3 **Area handbook for the peripheral states of the Arabian
peninsula.**
American University, Foreign Area Studies
Department. Washington, DC : US Government Printing
Office, 1971. 201p. 5 maps. bibliog.
Qatar is discussed in chapter 6, 'The Gulf states', of this introduction to the
region. It includes summaries of the physical environment, population, ethnic and
religious groups, social change and living conditions, political structure, economic
structure and the security forces.

1

The Country and Its People

4 **Background notes, Qatar.**
Washington, DC: US Department of State, Office of Public
Communications, Bureau of Public Affairs, 1979. 4p. 2 maps.
bibliog.
A regularly updated introduction to Qatar covering its geography, government
and political conditions, economy, defence, foreign relations, and travel notes.

5 **ABECOR country report: Qatar.**
Prepared by Barclays Bank Group Economics
Department. London: Barclays Bank, March 1981. 2p.
One of the series of irregularly updated country reports issued by the members of
the ABECOR European banks association. Covers the politics and economy of
Qatar, including sections on oil and gas, industry, finance, trade and the
medium-term outlook, which is seen as promising.

6 **Basic data on the economy of Bahrain, Qatar, Muscat and
Oman, and the Trucial States.**
Overseas Business Reports (US Department of Commerce),
vol. 22 (March 1968), p. 1-14.
The section on Qatar (p. 6-8) includes summaries of its geography, population,
government, economic structure, petroleum, agriculture, currency and banking,
development, foreign trade, and trade with the USA in the 1960s.

7 **Le Golfe persique: mer de légende - reservoir de pétrole.** (The
Persian Gulf: sea of legend - reservoir of oil.)
Jean-Jacques Berreby. Paris: Payot, 1959. 228p. 4 maps.
bibliog.
A general introduction to the Gulf in French. Qatar is particularly mentioned in
chapter 13 where its development following the discovery of oil is described as
frenetic. The growth of social services in Qatar in the form of education and
health facilities is praised.

8 **Who's who in the Arab world 1978-1979.**
Edited by Gabriel M. Bustros. Beirut: Publitec Publications,
1978. 5th ed. 2,058p.
Provides comprehensive coverage of historical, economic and political events in
the Middle East. Qatar is surveyed on p. 823-76, where information on the
country's geography, population, culture, history, government, constitution,
currency, industry, agriculture, education, welfare, economy and communications
is given.

9 The Persian Gulf states.
Edited by Alvin J. Cottrell, C. Edmund Bosworth, R. Michael
Burrell, Keith McLachlan, Roger M. Savory. Baltimore,
Maryland; London: Johns Hopkins University Press, 1980.
695p. 6 maps. bibliog.

This extremely detailed book treats the Gulf as a whole. It is divided into five
main sections: the history of the Gulf, economics and urban development, cultural
background, arts and society, and finally twelve appendixes. A number of chapters, in addition to providing general observations on the Gulf, are subdivided into
sections on each country within the region. Qatar is mentioned particularly in
connection with the oil industry, agriculture, urbanization, and education. The
appendixes provide a wealth of summarized information on such aspects as climate, flora, demography, industrial development, and the agricultural sector.
Each chapter and appendix has its own selected bibliography. It provides one of
the most comprehensive introductions to the wider region within which Qatar is a
small, but nevertheless important, element.

10 The Arab of the desert: a glimpse into Badawin life in Kuwait and Sau'di Arabia.
H. R. P. Dickson. London: George Allen & Unwin, 1949.
648p. 9 maps.

Qatar is mentioned in this description of bedouin life in connection with pearling
(chapter 38).

11 The oil states.
W. B. Fisher. London: Batsford Academic & Educational,
1980. 71p. 6 maps. (Today's World).

An introduction for schoolchildren to the geography, history, society, religion,
economy and politics of the oil states of the Middle East. Qatar, as one of the
smaller oil producers, is mentioned in scattered references throughout the book.

12 Qatar.
Bernard Gérard. Boulogne, France: Editions Delroisse, for
the Ministry of Information, Qatar [n.d.]. 180p.

An introduction to the history, culture, economy and society of Qatar. It includes
fine photographs of the country and its people.

13 Arabian time machine: self-portrait of an oil state.
Helga Graham. London: Heinemann, 1978. 338p. map.

A personal view of Qatar expressed through a series of interviews. It does not
claim to be scientific, historical or academic, and represents the views of those
involved in the pearl trade, the bedouin, the technocrats, old men, women veiled
and unveiled, the professionals, and youth. It concludes with two Western views
of Qatar, and, in contrast, several opinions of Qataris on the West.

The Country and Its People

14 **Iraq and the Persian Gulf.**
Great Britain. Admiralty, Naval Intelligence
Division. London: HM Stationery Office, 1944. 682p. 97
maps. (Geographical Handbook Series, B.R. 524).
Qatar's physical environment, towns and people are described on p. 139-41. Mention is also made of the oil concession granted to Petroleum Development (Qatar) Ltd.

15 **A handbook of Arabia.**
Great Britain. Admiralty War Staff, Intelligence
Division. London: HM Stationery Office, 1916-17. 2 vols.
5 maps.
Provides much useful information on the tribes of Arabia and their allegiances at the time of the First World War. Volume 1 is concerned with a physical and social survey of Arabia, and El-Qatar is discussed in detail in chapter 9. Descriptions are given of the towns and villages of Qatar, the physical environment, and the population at the beginning of the 20th century. Volume 2 provides information on communications and travel.

16 **The Arab states of the Persian Gulf and south-east Arabia.**
Great Britain. Central Office of Information, Reference
Division. London: HM Stationery Office, 1962. 28p. 3
maps. (R.5322).
This paper includes details of Britain's relations with the Persian Gulf area and information concerning each of the Arab states forming its littoral. Qatar is discussed on p. 22-23, with sections on the oil industry and socio-economic development.

17 **Persian Gulf states.**
David Holden. In: *The Middle East: a handbook*. Edited by
Michael Adams. London: Anthony Blond, 1971, p. 253-62.
Provides a basic introduction to the geography, history, politics, defence, internal preoccupations, external affairs and Great Power interests in the Gulf.

18 **Qatar into the seventies.**
Information Department, in collaboration with Frank
O'Shanohun Associates. Doha: Qatar National Printing
Press, 1970. 104p. 3 maps.
An introduction to Qatar covering the state, foreign affairs, the government, public security, the environment, the people, petroleum, education, welfare, agriculture, infrastructure, finance, commerce, and communications. It was written at a time when Qatar was, under Article 1 of the provisional constitution, a member of the Union of Arab Emirates.

19 **The international cookbook of Qatar.**
Doha: Ali Bin Ali Printing Press, 1977. 148p.
A book produced by the American women in Qatar as an aid to make shopping and cooking easier for US newcomers to the state, to introduce them to a selec-

tion of Arabic dishes typical of the Gulf region, and to help duplicate favourite US recipes with ingredients available in Qatar.

20 **The Gulf handbook 1976-77.**
Edited by Peter Kilner, Jonathan Wallace. Bath, England: Trade and Travel Publications, 1979. 3rd ed. 1,224p. 8p. of maps.
A guide to the Gulf for business travellers and other visitors. Qatar is discussed on p. 461-504, where information is provided on its history, constitution, geography, social background, tourism, education, health and housing, industry, trade, agriculture and fishing, oil, banking, finance and infrastructural development, in addition to sections on facts and figures and lists of hotels, embassies and banks.

21 **Qatar and its people.**
Chris Kutschera. *Africa*, no. 12 (1972), p. 73-78.
An account of the history and economy of Qatar from the 18th century. Most attention is paid to the political structure of the state and the development of the oil industry. It is interesting for the emphasis that it gives to the 'coup' in which Shaikh Khalifa bin Hamad removed his cousin Shaikh Ahmed Ben Ali Al-Thani as emir in February 1972.

22 **Emirats arabes du Golfe: Kowait-Bahrain-Qatar-Fédération des Emirats Unis.** (Arab emirates of the Gulf: Kuwait, Bahrain, Qatar, the Federation of United Emirates.)
Philippe Lannois. Geneva: Editions Nagel, 1976. 208p. 12 maps. bibliog.
This is a tourist encyclopaedia of the Gulf in French. After a general introduction covering the geography, population, customs, economy and ways of life in the area, each country is discussed in turn, with Qatar being surveyed on p. 117-40. Details are provided of Qatar's recent history, government administration, and economy, in addition to tourist hints on Doha and the remainder of the peninsula.

23 **Kuwait, Bahrain, Qatar, Oman, Arabemiraten. En guide för affarsmän och turister.** (Kuwait, Bahrain, Qatar, Oman and the United Arab Emirates. A guide for businessmen and tourists.)
Mark Lippold. Stockholm: Generalstabens Litografiska Anstalts Förlag, 1978. 286p. 7 maps.
Qatar is mainly discussed on p. 195-204 of this Swedish guide to the Gulf. Introductory sections provide general details on the economy and history of the area, as well as an A to Z of useful information for tourists. Aspects of Qatar's industry and culture are included.

The Country and Its People

24 **The Persian Gulf: an introduction to its peoples, politics, and economics.**
David E. Long. Boulder, Colorado: Westview Press, 1976. 172p. 2 maps. bibliog. (Westview Special Studies on the Middle East).
A broad survey of the Gulf, which concentrates mainly on politics, the significance of oil, and the relations of the region with the USA. Qatar is discussed specifically in the chapters on the land and people (p. 15-16), on the political dynamics of the Gulf states (p. 34-35), and on economic prospects in the Gulf (p. 119-20), and there are several other scattered references to the state.

25 **The Middle East and North Africa.**
London: Europa Publications, 1948- . annual.
After an introductory general survey and details of regional organizations, the countries of the Middle East are analysed in turn. Annually revised notes on Qatar cover its geography, history, and economy, and there is a section on statistics in addition to a directory of the state.

26 **Middle East Annual Review.**
Saffron Walden, England: Middle East Review, 1974- . annual.
After introductory sections on politics, trade, industry, civil engineering and construction, services, and finance in the Middle East, each country is surveyed in turn. The chapter on Qatar provides information on the political system, Gulf relations, agriculture, the manpower problem, heavy industry, development spending, oil income, banking, and infrastructure. Some statistics are also provided.

27 **The Middle East Yearbook.**
London: IC Magazines, 1977- . annual.
After two introductory sections on politics and society, and economy and business in the Middle East, this publication gives a country-by-country account of the region. The chapter on Qatar covers general information, political history, social and economic issues, current events, and statistics.

28 **In defiance of the elements: a personal view of Qatar.**
John Moorehead, photographs by Robin Constable. London: Quartet Books, 1977. 160p.
A general introduction to the history and contemporary culture of Qatar, with many photographs. The historical section includes discussions of piracy, Qatar's relationship with Bahrain, and the Turkish and British involvement. The part on Qatar today has subsections on the city of Doha, the pearl trade, merchants, civil servants, students, the desert, the bedouin, fishing, oil, agriculture and industry.

29 **Area handbook for the Persian Gulf states.**
Richard F. Nyrop (and others). Washington, DC: US Government Printing Office, 1977. 448p. 8 maps. bibliog.
This detailed handbook covers the countries of Bahrain, Kuwait, Qatar, Oman and the United Arab Emirates. It begins with five general chapters on the society, history, religion and oil industries of the region. Each country is then

considered in detail, with Qatar being discussed in chapter 8. Particular attention is paid to the physical environment, demography, the economy, political dynamics, foreign relations, mass communications, and defence.

30 The Gulf states and Oman.
Christine Osborne. London: Croom Helm, 1977. 208p. 5 maps. bibliog.

A journalistic account of recent socio-economic change in the Gulf. Chapter 3 discusses Qatar, and argues that Shaikh Khalifa is proceeding more cautiously than other rulers in the region. Within this chapter the following topics are summarized briefly: business and investment, education and housing, communications, hotels, and agriculture and wildlife. Two concluding chapters are concerned with the changing lifestyle of the bedouin and with 'the emerging women of the Gulf'.

31 Nomadism on the Arabian peninsula: a general appraisal.
P. G. N Peppelenbosch. Tijdschrift voor Economische en Sociale Geografie, vol. 59 (1968), p. 335-46.

A study of the increasing crisis of nomadism in Arabia. The poverty of pasture in the Gulf coastal region, including Qatar, is one reason why there are fewer nomads in this region than in other parts of the peninsula.

32 Qatar.
Doha: Ministry of Information [n.d.]. 32p.

Provides background information on government, the capital Doha, history, petroleum and allied projects, industrial diversification, agriculture, finance and trade, transport and communications, infrastructural development, education, health, hotels and restaurants, leisure activities and sports in Qatar.

33 Qatar.
Voice [of the Arab World], no. 53 (16 Sept. 1976), suppl., p. 5-20.

Published five years after Qatar's independence this provides an historical introduction to Qatar in addition to contemporary information on fishing, construction, agriculture, the economic transformation, education, industry and trade with Britain.

34 Qatar: a special report.
The Times (UK), 23 June 1975, p. I-X.

A thorough report on Qatar in the mid-1970s, including details on planning, the oil industry, the adoption of heavy industry, social development, political relations with neighbouring states, a government progress report in the form of an advertisement, the Qatar National Museum, nomadism, the herd of Arabian oryx on the Al-Zubara estate, education, agriculture and communications.

35 Qatar: a special report.
The Times (UK), 3 Sept. 1980, p. 19-24.

An assessment of the political and economic climate of Qatar, the world's third richest country per capita. In addition to a general assessment it includes specific sections on energy, gas, industry, banking, labour, communications and agriculture. Economic statistics and details of the government are included at the end of the report.

36 Qatar: a special report.
The Times (UK), 31 March 1982, p. I-IV

An account of the changes that have taken place in Qatar over the last ten years, and the prospects over the next decade. Particular attention is paid to the North Field gas deposits, which are said to be the world's largest single concentration of non-associated gas reserves. There are also sections on oil, banking, industry, business, and the capital Doha. A short concluding guide for visitors notes the hotels available in the country.

37 Qatar: facts and figures.
Doha: Ministry of Information, Press and Publications Department, 1980. 17p.

A brief introduction to Qatar covering its geography, historical background, economic development, social development, tourism and culture, concluding with a section on general information.

38 Qatar 1968.
Qatar Government. London: Frank O'Shanohun Associates, 1968. 95p. 2 maps.

A useful introduction to the social and economic structure of Qatar as it was towards the end of the 1960s. It is particularly interesting in an historical context, since it provides a summary point from which more recent developments can be evaluated. The most detailed information within it is related to the oil industry. A list of the government of Qatar in March 1968 is recorded on p. 18-19.

39 Qatar progress II.
Doha: Ministry of Education, Cultural Relations Department, 1964. 71p. 2 maps.

Provides information on the geography, government machinery, legislative development, financial and economic affairs, human activities, petroleum, education, government departments, social services, and social life in Qatar in the mid-1960s.

40 Qatar today.
Doha: Ministry of Information [n.d.]. 103p.

A well-illustrated introduction to Qatar, published on the occasion of the forty-eighth Ministerial Conference of OPEC held in Doha. It includes sections on the history, the state government, public services, social services, and economy of Qatar.

41 Qatar Year Book 1978-79.
Doha: Ministry of Information, Press and Publications Department [n.d.]. 204p. map.

An account of Qatar's recent development. The introduction covers Qatar's geography, history and people. This is followed by sections on the state, social services, public services, and the economy. It concludes with ninety tables covering most aspects of the economy.

42 **Arabia through the looking glass.**
Jonathan Raban. London: Collins, 1979. 348p.
The story of the author's travels in Bahrain, Qatar, the United Arab Emirates, Yemen, Egypt and Jordan. Life in Doha, a fishing trip, and conversations with people living in Qatar are included.

43 **Tribal areas and migration lines of the north Arabian bedouins.**
Carl R. Raswan. *American Geographical Review*, vol. 20 (1930), p. 494-502.
This paper on the *diras* (tribal pasture districts) of northern Arabia notes that Qatar lay in the *dira* of the Beni Hajr and was also used during certain seasons by the 'Ajman.

44 **Die arabische Halbinsel: Saudi-Arabien, Yemen, Südyemen, Kuwait, Bahrain, Qatar, Vereinigte Arabische Emirate, Oman; Reiseführer mit Landeskunde.** (The Arabian peninsula: Saudi Arabia, Yemen, South Yemen, Kuwait, Bahrain, Qatar, United Arab Emirates, Oman; guidebook with national studies.)
Wigand Ritter. Buchenhain vor München, GFR: Volk und Heimat, 1978. 278p. 20 maps.
A German handbook on Arabia. Qatar is discussed on p. 206-16. It provides some general information on the state's geography, history and economy, and includes some practical advice for residents.

45 **Gazetteer of Arabia: a geographical and tribal history of the Arabian peninsula. Volume 1.**
Edited by Sheila A. Scoville. Graz, Austria: Akademische Druck-u. Verlagsanstalt, 1979. 733p.
This is an extremely detailed volume based on the 1917 British gazetteer of Arabia. It covers entries from letters A to E, including, for example, three pages on Doha. The work will be complete in four volumes.

46 **Arabian Studies.**
Edited by R. B. Serjeant, R. L. Bidwell. London: C. Hurst & Co.; Totowa, New Jersey: Rowman & Littlefield, 1974- . annual.
A multi-disciplinary journal covering all aspects of the Arabian peninsula.

The Country and Its People

47 **Special report: Qatar.**
Commerce International, April 1977, p. 45-71.
Provides information on Qatar's economic development, Anglo-Qatari trade, infrastructure, agriculture, oil and gas industry, banking, and the 1977 budget. It suggests that Qatar remains one of the least known of the Arab countries among British businessmen, and that the country has taken a more prudent approach to spending its oil revenue than have many other Arab states.

48 **Spotlight Qatar.**
London: Midland Bank International, June 1979. (Spotlight no. 155).
Gives details of the country, economy, market opportunities, and import requirements of Qatar.

49 **State of Qatar.**
Doha: Ministry of Information, Press and Publications Department [n.d.]. 20p. map.
An introduction to Qatar, which provides information on the ruling Al-Thani family, the religion of Islam, the desert, the Ministry of Information, oil, industrial diversification, commerce, and the youth of the nation in the late 1970s. Six cards at the back of the publication cover the Ras Abu Fontas power station and desalination plant, Umm Said, Qatari-British relations, social development, Hamad General Hospital, and some general information.

50 **The central Middle East: a handbook of anthropology.**
Edited by Louise E. Sweet. New Haven, Connecticut: Human Relations Area Files, 1968. 2 vols. bibliogs.
Qatar is mentioned in chapter 4 of this series of anthropological essays.

51 **This is Qatar.**
Doha: Gulf Public Relations, 1978- . quarterly.
Each issue contains approximately half-a-dozen articles, on subjects ranging from falconry and natural history to the development of education and traditional Qatari dress. In addition there is a section on general information in each issue, which includes maps of Qatar and its capital Doha.

52 **Les émirats du golfe Arabe: le Koweït, Bahreïn, Qatar et les Emirats Arabes Unis.** (The Arabian Gulf emirates: Kuwait, Bahrain, Qatar and the United Arab Emirates.)
Jean-Jacques L. Tur. Paris: Presses Universitaires de France, 1976. 125p. 10 maps. bibliog. (Que Sais-je?).
An introduction to the Gulf in French. It provides basic information on the history and geography of the region, and the revolution brought about by oil. The final chapters discuss the two sets of alternatives of diversity or tribalism, and solidarity or federalism. Qatar is mentioned in particular on p. 81-83, but there are frequent other mentions of the state.

1971-1981: a decade of progress.
See item no. 242.

Geography and Geology

53 The study of and a contribution to the geomorphology of the Arabian Gulf.

Taiba A. Al-Asfour. In: *Change and development in the Middle East: essays in honour of W. B. Fisher.* Edited by John I. Clarke, Howard Bowen-Jones. London, New York: Methuen, 1981, p. 173-88.

This is a useful summary of the research undertaken on the Gulf. It notes that calcareous sandstone raised beaches occur in Qatar, suggesting that there was a Pleistocene sea-level at a height of about 25-30 metres. Comment is also passed on Houbolt's identification of four submarine terrace-like levels to the north and east of the Qatar peninsula.

54 Water resources and their management in the Middle East.

Peter Beaumont. In: *Change and development in the Middle East: essays in honour of W. B. Fisher.* Edited by John I. Clarke, Howard Bowen-Jones. London, New York: Methuen, 1981, p. 40-72.

This paper includes a discussion of desalinated water production in Qatar which, it notes, dates back to 1954. It is current government policy to ensure that water demand is met by desalinated water production. There are also plans to recharge the fresh groundwater lens with desalinated water.

55 The Middle East: a geographical study.

Peter Beaumont, Gerald H. Blake, J. Malcolm Wagstaff. London: John Wiley & Sons, 1976. 572p. 100 maps. bibliog.

An extensive introduction to the Middle East with scattered references to Qatar, particularly on the subject of economic growth resulting from oil revenue.

Geography and Geology

56 **The petroleum geology and resources of the Middle East.**
Z. R. Beydoun, H. V. Dunnington. Beaconsfield, England:
Scientific Press, 1975. 99p. 5 maps. bibliog.
This book provides a synopsis of the geology of the Middle East, including details
of stratigraphy, structure and geological evolution. Qatar's oilfields are discussed
on p. 39, and details of its stratigraphy are provided on p. 59-60.

57 **The environmental history of the Near and Middle East since
the last Ice Age.**
Edited by William C. Brice. London, New York: Academic
Press, 1978. 384p. 55 maps.
A collection of twenty-two papers on the environmental history of the Middle
East, most of which have their own lists of references. Qatar is briefly mentioned
in the papers by Larsen and Evans, Al-Asfour, and Vita-Finzi in connection with
sea-level changes, and also by Stevens in a discussion of the salt flats known as
sabkha.

58 **Geological description of the Qatar peninsula (Arabian Gulf).**
Claude Cavelier. Paris: Bureau de Recherches Géologiques
et Minières, for the Government of Qatar, Department of
Petroleum Affairs, 1970. 39p. 3 maps. bibliog.
This description of the geology of Qatar is divided into six main sections: previous
geological publications, which are few in number; the existing geological maps;
the Tertiary stratigraphy, subdivided into discussions of the Palaeogene:Hasa
series, and the Neogene; the Quaternary and superficial deposits, with sections on
marine deposits, continental deposits, and marine deposits subjected to continental
evolution, such as the *sabkha*; the major structural surface features; and the
palaeographical history of Qatar during the Tertiary. There are also brief discussions on the general geography of Qatar, and on the geology of the offshore
islands. In conclusion Qatar is seen as an elliptic-shaped giant anticline, with a
north-south main axis, outlined by outcrops of Eocene rocks, essentially without
their more recent cover. It is not a simple structure, and is limited to the west by
a long, narrow fold corresponding to the Djebel Dukhan.

59 **Geological survey and mineral substances exploration in Qatar
(Arabian Gulf).**
Claude Cavelier. Paris: Bureau de Recherches Géologiques
et Minières, for the Government of Qatar, Department of
Petroleum Affairs, 1970. 100p. bibliog.
The report of a reconnaissance to evaluate the mineral potential of Qatar. It is
divided into four main sections: a brief description of the main general features of
Qatar; a detailed geological description of the peninsula; a geological description
of the offshore islands; and a summary of the mineral resources of Qatar. The
main minerals other than oil, natural gas and fresh water are: white crystalline
limestone, green calcareous clay, Quaternary marine calcareous sand, recrystal-
lized limestone and superficial dolomites. Minerals of secondary importance are:
siliceous-calcareous eolian sand, Quaternary beach gravels, depression silts and
muds, and salt from the *sabkha*. Gypsum is very abundant locally on the surface
of Qatar. No major deposits of iron or phosphate were discovered. The report
considers that the most promising field is the existence of elements to be found in
the salt waters surrounding the state.

Geography and Geology

60 Change and development in the Middle East: essays in honour of W. B. Fisher.
Edited by John I. Clarke, Howard Bowen-Jones. London, New York: Methuen, 1981. 322p. 26 maps.

A collection of essays by staff and research students of the Department of Geography of Durham University, England, as a festschrift in honour of the retiring head of department, Professor W. B. Fisher. It concentrates on the changes that have taken place in the Middle East over the last thirty years. The papers by Bowen-Jones, Beaumont, McLachlan, Blake, Clarke, Al-Asfour and Donaldson make particular reference to Qatar.

61 Organisms as producers of carbonate sediment and indicators of environment in the southern Persian Gulf.
M. W. Hughes Clarke, A. J. Keij. In: *The Persian Gulf: holocene carbonate sedimentation and diagenesis in a shallow epicontinental sea.* Edited by B. H. Purser. Berlin; Heidelberg, GFR; New York: Springer-Verlag, 1973, p. 33-56.

Planktonic faunas are scarce in the Gulf sediments. Nectonic animals are also scarce, but benthonic life is abundant. Increasing restriction seems to be clearest where salinities attain fifty grams per litre. Imperforate foraminifera are the dominant assemblage near Qatar.

62 Fractured reservoirs of Middle East.
E. J. Daniel. *American Association of Petroleum Geologists Bulletin*, vol. 38, pt. 5 (1954), p. 774-815.

This paper describes the reservoirs of three oilfields, Ain Zalah and Kirkuk in Iraq, and Dukhan in Qatar. In the Dukhan field the limestones are generally moderately to highly porous and permeable. The effect of jointing is minor and the maximum rate of flow of individual wells is less than that from the two Iraqi fields.

63 Water resources and land use in the Qatīf oasis of Saudi Arabia.
Charles H. V. Ebert. *Geographical Review*, vol. 55 (1965), p. 496-509.

Qatar, lying to the east of Al Qatīf, is seen as forming part of the Miocene-Pliocene complex in which that town is found.

64 Oxford regional economic atlas: the Middle East and North Africa.
Economist Intelligence Unit, Clarendon Press Cartographic Department. Oxford, England: Oxford University Press, 1960. 135p. 64p. of maps. bibliog.

Includes maps on agriculture, oil, industries, and communications, in addition to general geographical and geological maps. Qatar is also mentioned in the section on supplementary notes and statistics that concludes the volume.

13

Geography and Geology

65 **Géographie d'Edrisi.** (Edrisi's geography.)
Abou-Abd-allah-Mohammed ben-Mohammed el-Edrisi,
translated from the Arabic by P. Amédée Jaubert. Paris:
Imprimerie Royale, 1836-40. 2 vols. 3 maps.
The Sea of Kithr (Qatar) is mentioned near Bahreïn in volume 1, p. 157, of this geography published in Arabic in Rome in 1592 and in Latin in Paris in 1619. The work was finished by the Arab geographer Abou-Abd-allah-Mohammed ben-Mohammed el-Edrisi in AD 1154. Only three of the original sixty-nine maps are included in this edition.

66 **Effluent re-use: how the Gulf states balance benefits and risks.**
World Water, Jan. 1981, p. 32-35.
Records that some municipal areas of Doha have been irrigated with treated effluent since the 1950s, and gives details of future plans.

67 **Sediments and water of Persian Gulf.**
K. O. Emery. *American Association of Petroleum Geologists Bulletin*, vol. 40, pt. 2 (1956), p. 2,354-83.
An evaluation of the findings of a two-week survey of the sediments and water characteristics of the Gulf undertaken in 1948. Qatar is surrounded mostly by sand, although there is some coral on its northern coast.

68 **The precipitation of aragonite and its alteration to calcite on the Trucial Coast of the Persian Gulf.**
B. D. Evamy. In: *The Persian Gulf: holocene carbonate sedimentation and diagenesis in a shallow epicontinental sea.*
Edited by B. H. Purser. Berlin; Heidelberg, GFR; New York: Springer-Verlag, 1973, p. 329-42.
Algal mats with irregularly aligned ridges are found in the Sabkha Faishakh area of Qatar. Aragonite is believed to be precipitating actively in certain of the sandy intertidal zones in response to the direct evaporation of marine water.

69 **Persian Gulf.**
Graham Evans. In: *Encyclopedia of oceanography.* Edited by R. W. Fairbridge. New York: Reinhold Publishing Corporation, 1966, p. 689-95.
A summary of the oceanography of the Gulf, in which it is recorded that the tides in the Gulf are lowest, around 4.0-5.4 feet, near Qatar.

70 **The recent sedimentary facies of the Persian Gulf region.**
Graham Evans. *Philosophical Transactions of the Royal Society of London*, series A, vol. 259 (1965-66), p. 291-98.
The Gulf is seen as an excellent model for the interpretation of the older deposits of the Middle East.

71 **Origin of the coastal flats, the sabkha of the Trucial Coast, Persian Gulf.**
Graham Evans, C. G. S. C. Kendall, P. A. d'E. Skipworth. *Nature* (UK), no. 4934, vol. 202 (May 1964), p. 759-61.
A discussion of the *sabkha* stretching from Ras Ghanada, near Abu Dhabi, to the eastern edge of Qatar.

72 **The Middle East: a physical, social and regional geography.**
W. B. Fisher. London: Methuen, 1978. 7th ed. 615p. 142 maps. bibliog.
This comprehensive book is divided into three main sections on the physical, the social and the regional geographies of the Middle East. Qatar is mentioned in chapter 16 on the Arabian peninsula, and is discussed as an example of a state that has undergone rapid change as a result of the exploitation of petroleum.

73 **Soil map of the world 1:5,000,000. Volume 7: South Asia.**
Food and Agriculture Organization. Paris: Unesco, 1977. 117p. 8 maps.
In addition to a soil map and maps of the regional divisions of climate, vegetation, geology, geomorphology and lithology of the Indian subcontinent and Arabian peninsula, this useful volume provides information on environmental conditions and land use and soil capability.

74 **Water resources in the Arab Middle East and North Africa.**
Christiaan E. Gischler. Cambridge, England: Middle East and North African Studies Press, 1979. 132p. 7 maps. bibliog.
A useful study of water resources and management in the Middle East. Qatar is used as a detailed example of water resources in the Gulf coastal area (p. 81-92), and a summary of the state's water balance statistics is provided on p. 108-10. A fresh water lens floats on the Palaeocene Umm er Radhuma formation under Qatar, and this lens is maintained almost entirely by stormwater run-off recharge. Information is provided on Qatar's agriculture and sea-water distillation programme. The author argues for a desalination programme to solve Qatar's water problems.

75 **The chemistry of submarine cement formation at Dohat Hussain in the Persian Gulf.**
K. de Groot. *Sedimentology*, vol. 12, no. 1-2 (1969), p. 63-68.
Results from a chemical study made at Dohat Hussain lagoon, on the west coast of Qatar, support evidence suggesting that submarine carbonate cementation is probably active there today, with the supersaturated lagoon water providing the source of the cement. Just below the sediment-water interface the presence of a stable substrate and supersaturation was found to promote aragonite precipitation.

76 **Geochemistry of tidal flat brines at Umm Said, S.E. Qatar, Persian Gulf.**
K. de Groot. In: *The Persian Gulf: holocene carbonate sedimentation and diagenesis in a shallow epicontinental sea.* Edited by B. H. Purser. Berlin; Heidelberg, GFR; New York: Springer-Verlag, 1973, p. 377-94.
An analysis of the seven-kilometre wide *sabkha* at Umm Said, in the south-east of Qatar. Both a reflux system and recent dolomite formation occur in this tidal flat.

77 **The Persian Gulf states and their boundary problems.**
Rupert Hay. *Geographical Journal*, vol. 120 (1954), p. 433-45.
A brief geographical description of the ten shaikhdoms on the southern coast of the Gulf as they were in the 1950s, with particular reference to the problems to which their boundaries gave rise. Qatar is described as possibly the ugliest stretch of territory that God has created.

78 **Surface sediments in the Persian Gulf near the Qatar peninsula.**
Jacob Jozef Herman Christiaan Houbolt. The Hague: Mouton, 1957. 113p. 11 maps. bibliog.
An analysis of the physiography and sedimentology of the Gulf near Qatar. Skeletal particles derived mainly from molluscs are found throughout the coastal areas of the Gulf. These skeletal particles are broken into finer debris by organic activity, and in zones of strong wave action the particles are rounded and transported in suspension to calmer areas. Below zones of wave activity the finer particles remain *in situ.* In the central Gulf area at depths of over forty fathoms skeletal particles over fifty-three microns in size tend not to be formed, and as a result marls tend to predominate. A speculative hypothesis is proposed to explain the morphology of the sea-bed near Qatar.

79 **Some geographical aspects of Qatar.**
T. M. Johnstone, J. C. Wilkinson. *Geographical Journal*, vol. 126, pt. 4 (Dec. 1960), p. 442-50.
A summary of the early literature and maps concerning Qatar, in addition to the tribes and geology of the peninsula.

80 **The structural and geomorphic evolution of the Persian Gulf.**
P. Kassler. In: *The Persian Gulf: holocene carbonate sedimentation and diagenesis in a shallow epicontinental sea.* Edited by B. H. Purser. Berlin; Heidelberg, GFR; New York: Springer-Verlag, 1973, p. 11-32.
The Gulf is a tectonic basin of late Pliocene to Pleistocene age. Pleistocene sedimentation subdued the tectonically controlled morphology, but was locally rejuvenated by Quaternary adjustments. In the Pleistocene the sea-level fell by 120 metres. The post-glacial Flandrian marine transgression began about 18,000 years BP.

81 **Mapping Arabia.**

John Leatherdale, Roy Kennedy. *Geographical Journal*, vol. 141, no. 2 (1975), p. 240-51.

This paper describes the survey techniques and methods of operation in the desert, paying particular attention to the work of Hunting Surveys. Mention is made of the geodetic network of first order traversing and levelling, aerial photography and the construction of a new set of topographical maps at a 1:50,000 scale for Qatar.

82 **The physical geography of south-eastern Arabia.**

G. M. Lees. *Geographical Journal*, vol. 71, no. 5 (May 1928), p. 441-70.

Appendix 2 of this paper is devoted to Qatar. The author claims to have been the second European, Burchardt being the first, to traverse the peninsula. The country is described as being 'monotonous to the extreme', and as being composed almost entirely of a horizontal Middle Eocene limestone sheet. There are other interesting pieces of information on Doha and Ibn Saud's *Ikhwan.*

83 **Recent movements in the Middle East.**

G. M. Lees. *Geologische Rundschau*, vol. 43, pt. 1 (1955), p. 221-26.

An investigation into the advance of the head of the Persian Gulf. Qatar is indicated on a general map, where its geology is noted as being Palaeogene and Mesozoic.

84 **Distribution and ultrastructure of holocene ooids in the Persian Gulf.**

J.-P. Loreau, B. H. Purser. In: *The Persian Gulf: holocene carbonate sedimentation and diagenesis in a shallow epicontinental sea.* Edited by B. H. Purser. Berlin; Heidelberg, GFR; New York: Springer-Verlag, 1973, p. 279-328.

Although most ooids are formed in agitated environments, significant quantities are also found within lagoons on the south-east lee coast of Qatar around Umm Said.

85 **Natural resources and development in the Gulf states.**

Keith McLachlan. In: *Social and economic development in the Arab Gulf.* Edited by Tim Niblock. London: Croom Helm, 1980, p. 80-94.

A summary of the physical resources of the Arab Gulf states.

86 **Political geography of Trucial Oman and Qatar.**

Alexander Melamid. *Geographical Review*, vol. 43, no. 2 (1953), p. 194-206.

A discussion of the physical and historical background of the region and of the early impact of oil development. The 19th century relationships between Qatar,

17

Geography and Geology

Bahrein, Great Britain and Turkey are mentioned, together with details of oil exploitation in the early 1950s.

87 **State of Qatar Ministry of Industry and Agriculture Integrated Water and Land Use Project, technical note no. 24: rainfall and groundwater recharge over Qatar.**
John G. Pike, Ibrahim Harhash, Brian A. P. Gemmell. Rome: United Nations Development Programme, with the Food and Agriculture Organization, 1975. 22p. 10 maps.

This paper shows that annual rainfall totals in Qatar conform to a log-normal frequency distribution. Annual recharge varies from seven to ten per cent of the annual rainfall and has amounted to 25 million cubic metres per annum over the four years prior to the report. The paper concludes that the present rate of over-exploitation of groundwater resources can only give rise to disquiet.

88 **The geology of the Persian Gulf and the adjoining portions of Persia and Arabia.**
G. E. Pilgrim. *Memoirs of the Geological Survey of India*, vol. 34, pt. 4 (1908), p. 1-177.

An account of the geology of the Gulf as it was known in the early 20th century. Qatar is briefly mentioned, but, unlike Bahrein, it is not discussed in great detail. Part 3, on the economic geology of the area, is of historical interest as an early evaluation of the petroleum potential of the Gulf.

89 **The Persian Gulf: holocene carbonate sedimentation and diagenesis in a shallow epicontinental sea.**
Edited by B. H. Purser. Berlin; Heidelberg, GFR; New York: Springer-Verlag, 1973. 474p. 3 maps. bibliog.

Twenty-two papers on holocene sedimentation and diagenesis in the Gulf.

90 **Sedimentation around bathymetric highs in the southern Persian Gulf.**
B. H. Purser. In: *The Persian Gulf: holocene carbonate sedimentation and diagenesis in a shallow epicontinental sea.* Edited by B. H. Purser. Berlin; Heidelberg, GFR; New York: Springer-Verlag, 1973, p. 157-78.

In this paper on the bathymetric highs of the Gulf, Halat Dalma shoal off the east coast of Qatar is described as an example of a relatively wide, locally emergent, intermediate homocline, which is constantly being swept by the north-north-west wind-driven waves and surface currents.

91 **Regional sedimentation along the Trucial Coast, SE Persian Gulf.**
B. H. Purser, G. Evans. In: *The Persian Gulf: holocene carbonate sedimentation and diagenesis in a shallow epicontinental sea.* Edited by B. H. Purser. Berlin; Heidelberg, GFR; New York: Springer-Verlag, 1973, p. 211-32.

The Qatar peninsula is identified as being an up-wind barrier influencing the sediment composition, surface patterns, and vertical sequences along the Trucial Coast, particularly in the west.

92 **Aragonitic, supratidal encrustations on the Trucial Coast, Persian Gulf.**
B. H. Purser, J.-P. Loreau. In: *The Persian Gulf: holocene carbonate sedimentation and diagenesis in a shallow epicontinental sea.* Edited by B. H. Purser. Berlin; Heidelberg, GFR; New York: Springer-Verlag, 1973, p. 343-76.

Strontium-rich aragonite crusts are well developed in protected lagoonal settings on the Trucial Coast. Examples of aragonitic encrustations can be found in Qatar at Umm Said and Khor Odaid.

93 **The principal environmental factors influencing holocene sedimentation and diagenesis in the Persian Gulf.**
B. H. Purser, E. Seibold. In: *The Persian Gulf: holocene carbonate sedimentation and diagenesis in a shallow epicontinental sea.* Edited by B. H. Purser. Berlin; Heidelberg, GFR; New York: Springer-Verlag, 1973, p. 1-10.

A summary of the physical environment of the Gulf, which consists of two major geological provinces: the stable Arabian foreland, and the unstable Iranian fold belt. Abnormally high salinities are caused by evaporation and partial isolation from the Indian Ocean. The Gulf has an average depth of 35 metres and a maximum depth of 100 metres near its entrance.

94 **Recent anhydrite, gypsum, dolomite, and halite from the coastal flats of the Arabian shore of the Persian Gulf.**
D. J. Shearman. *Proceedings of the Geological Society of London,* no. 1607 (2 July 1963), p. 63-64.

An investigation into the content of the *sebkha* of the Arabian coast of the Gulf. It mentions that dolomite has been found around Qatar.

95 **Carbonate coastal accretion in an area of longshore transport, NE Qatar, Persian Gulf.**
E. A. Shinn. In: *The Persian Gulf: holocene carbonate sedimentation and diagenesis in a shallow epicontinental sea.* Edited by B. H. Purser. Berlin; Heidelberg, GFR; New York: Springer-Verlag, 1973, p. 179-92.
Sedimentation in an eighteen-kilometre long and seven-kilometre wide area of north-east Qatar between Khor and Ras Laffan is described. Chenier beach and spit development has straightened the coast.

96 **Recent intertidal and nearshore carbonate sedimentation around rock highs, E. Qatar, Persian Gulf.**
E. A. Shinn. In: *The Persian Gulf: holocene carbonate sedimentation and diagenesis in a shallow epicontinental sea.* Edited by B. H. Purser. Berlin; Heidelberg, GFR; New York: Springer-Verlag, 1973, p. 193-98.
Low mesa-like hills of Tertiary dolomite and limestone, protruding through intertidal and supratidal sediments, characterize much of the terrestrial morphology of eastern Qatar.

97 **Sedimentary accretion along the leeward, SE coast of Qatar peninsula, Persian Gulf.**
E. A. Shinn. In: *The Persian Gulf: holocene carbonate sedimentation and diagenesis in a shallow epicontinental sea.* Edited by B. H. Purser. Berlin; Heidelberg, GFR; New York: Springer-Verlag, 1973, p. 199-210.
South of Umm Said north-west *shamal* winds have piled up quartz dunes which are migrating into the sea prograding the coast and producing a quartz sand *sabkha.*

98 **Submarine lithification of holocene carbonate sediments in the Persian Gulf.**
E. A. Shinn. *Sedimentology*, vol. 12, no. 1-2 (1969), p. 109-44.
Studies from the Zekrit and Dohat Hussain lagoons, both in Qatar, together with evidence from other parts of the Gulf, illustrate that cementation is occurring within the present submarine environment. The chemistry of the processes is unknown, but it would seem only to require carbonate-saturated sea-water. The principal physical factors involved appear to be relatively low rates of sedimentation, sediment stability, and high initial permeability of the sediment.

99 **Lower Tertiary foraminifera of the Qatar peninsula.**
Alan Hilder Smout. Norwich, England: Jarrold & Sons, for the British Museum, 1954. 96p. bibliog.
This book discusses the basic structure of the test in foraminifera of the super-family Rotaliicea, and revises the family Rotaliidae. It includes an introduction to the geology and stratigraphy of Qatar. The country forms part of a large, gently

anticlinal area, and its lithology is dominantly calcareous marls. There are fifteen plates and forty-four figures illustrating the fossils identified.

100 **Some aspects of sedimentation in the Persian Gulf.**
W. Sugden. *Journal of Sedimentary Petrology*, vol. 33, no. 2 (1963), p. 355-64.
A report on the sedimentology of the Gulf. High levels of chlorinity are noted to the west of Qatar. On the east coast of the country true oöliths are found in the foreset sands, but on the west coast only pseudo-oöliths are reported. The sea area west of Qatar is noted as being very shallow with bottomset sediments in some areas consisting mainly of muds.

101 **Holocene intertidal calcium carbonate cementation, Qatar, Persian Gulf.**
J. C. M. Taylor, L. V. Illing. *Sedimentology*, vol. 12, no. 1-2 (1969), p. 69-107.
Cemented layers in the shallow lagoonal intertidal and supratidal sediments surrounding Qatar are shown to contain high-magnesian calcite and aragonite cements. The magnesian calcite occurs both as a primary precipitate and also as a replacement of aragonite. Two types of cemented layer are described: one is approximately one metre thick in the form of variably cemented bed rock at the surface of beaches, the other is a few centimetres thick and is found beneath the surface of intertidal sand flats. Radiocarbon dates provide an upper age limit for the cements of about 4,500 years.

102 **Arabia in early maps: a bibliography of maps covering the peninsula of Arabia in western Europe from the invention of printing to the year 1751.**
G. R. Tibbetts. Naples, Italy: Falcon Press; New York; Cambridge, England: Oleander Press, 1978. 175p. 22 maps. bibliog.
It is interesting to note that Qatar is not illustrated with any accuracy on any of the maps depicted within this volume.

103 **Environmental history.**
C. Vita-Finzi. In: *Qatar archaeological report: excavations 1973*. Edited by Beatrice de Cardi. Oxford, England: Oxford University Press, 1978, p. 11-25.
A summary of the work undertaken on the evolution of the coasts and internal basins of Qatar during the period of human occupancy. It concludes that between 70,000 and 44,000 BP the floor of the Arabian Gulf was dry land. There then appears to have ensued a period of about 14,000 years when there was flooding of the Gulf, which endowed Qatar with readily accessible coastal resources. A second fall in the sea-level attained its maximum in 15,000 BP. Basin-filling created a set of resources which complemented the coastal food supply and permitted year-round occupation, possibly based on seasonal migration between the littoral and the interior. Silt deposition during the Islamic period enabled permanent settlement to take place in favoured depressions where dams were constructed to promote the accumulation of alluvium and the infiltration of flood run-off.

21

104 **Holocene sediment types and their distribution in the southern Persian Gulf.**
C. W. Wagner, C. Van der Togt. In: *The Persian Gulf: holocene carbonate sedimentation and diagenesis in a shallow epicontinental sea.* Edited by B. H. Purser. Berlin; Heidelberg, GFR; New York: Springer-Verlag, 1973, p. 123-56.

Fourteen major units of the holocene sediments are identified based on textures and grain type. Towards the centre of the basin of the sea floor there is increased protection from wave action, and the sediments therefore grade from skeletal, oolitic and pelletoidal sands and fringing reefs, through irregular compound grain sands, into basin centre muds.

105 **Some ideas on winter atmospheric processes over south-west Asia.**
J. M. Walker. *Meteorological Magazine,* vol. 96 (1967), p. 161-67.

This paper analyses the weather of south-west Asia in relation to the subtropical and polar front jet streams. It is one of the few papers discussing the weather in the region of which Qatar forms a part.

106 **Recent dolomite in the Persian Gulf.**
Alan J. Wells. *Nature* (UK), no. 4825, vol. 194 (April 1962), p. 274-75.

Current report of the Koninklijke/Shell Exploratie en Produktie Laboratorium in association with V. C. Illing & Partners study of recent carbonates in the Qatar area. It notes that the proportion of aragonite in the carbonate sediment rises to ninety-five per cent or more on some of the algal flats just below the level of diurnal high tide. Dolomite and gypsum are seen as being derived from sea-water left behind in the sediment on the upper part of the tidal flats and concentrated by evaporation during the time between spring or storm tides.

Boundaries and petroleum developments in southern Arabia.
See item no. 329.

Oil and the evolution of boundaries in eastern Arabia.
See item no. 330.

Political boundaries and nomadic grazing.
See item no. 331.

Plans underway to make Qatar a major source of petroleum.
See item no. 478.

Water resources and agriculture in Qatar.
See item no. 488.

Travel and Exploration

107 **Travellers in Arabia.**
Robin Leonard Bidwell.   London: Hamlyn, 1976. 224p.
bibliog.
A selection of the travels undertaken by Europeans in Arabia. Qatar is mentioned
in connection with Palgrave's visit to the peninsula in 1863, although some doubts
are cast on the integrity of his report. The book includes a number of interesting
photographs.

108 **Ost-Arabien von Basra bis Maskat auf Grund, eigener Reisen.**
(East Arabia from Basra to Maskat - my own journey by
land.)
Von Hermann Bürchardt.   *Zeitschrift der Gesellschaft fur
Erdkunde zu Berlin,* 1906, p. 305-22.
The account of the author's journey across eastern Arabia from Kuwait through
Bahrain, Hufuf, Abu Thubby, Dobbay and Râs El Chême to Maskat.

109 **Explorers of Arabia from the Renaissance to the end of the
Victorian era.**
Zahra Freeth, H. V. F. Winstone.   London: George Allen
& Unwin, 1978. 308p. 11 maps. bibliog.
This mentions Palgrave's journey to Qatar in January 1863. There he transferred
into a different ship hoping to go on to Oman.

23

Travel and Exploration

110 **The penetration of Arabia: a record of the development of Western knowledge concerning the Arabian peninsula.**
David George Hogarth. London: Alston Rivers, 1905. 359p. 20 maps.

One of the first major volumes describing the exploration of inland Arabia. The omission of Katar from D'Anville's map of 1755 is noted, and it is mentioned that Katar was at the southern end of Turkish control in Arabia.

111 **Narrative of a year's journey through central and eastern Arabia (1862-63).**
William Gifford Palgrave. London; Cambridge, England: Macmillan, 1865. 2 vols. Reprinted, Farnborough, England: Gregg International, 1969.

Katar is discussed in chapter 14 of this record of Palgrave's journey across Arabia. He stayed in Bedaa', which he describes as the miserable capital of a miserable province, and he notes a large number of castles in the country built to defend the wealth derived from pearl fishing. He was of the opinion that four days were fairly sufficient for knowing all that was worth knowing about Katar.

112 **Arabian days.**
H. St. John B. Philby. London: Robert Hale, 1948. 336p.

Philby's autobiography, which mentions Qatar briefly as the end point of Thomas's crossing of the Rub' al Khali.

113 **A la découverte de l'Arabie: cinq siècles de science et d'aventure.** (On the discovery of Arabia: five centuries of science and adventure.)
Jacqueline Pirenne. Paris: Livre Contemporain, 1958. 328p. 7 maps. bibliog.

A study of the European discovery of Arabia. It points out that D'Anville's map of 1755, which was the first approximately accurate map of Arabia to be produced, failed to show the peninsula of Qatar.

114 **Around the coasts of Arabia.**
Ameen Rihani. London: Constable, 1930. 364p.

Qatar is briefly mentioned in the section on Bahrain of this book of the author's travels in, and reminiscences of, Arabia.

115 **Arabian adventure.**
Anthony Shepherd. London: Collins, 1961. 256p. map.

A record of the eighteen months spent by the author with the Trucial Oman Scouts between 1957-59. It notes, in passing, the road along the southern coast of the Gulf from Sharjah to Qatar, and it includes several other scattered references to Qatar.

116 **The travels of Pedro Teixeira with his 'Kings of Harmuz' and extracts from his 'Kings of Persia'.**
Translated and annotated by William F. Sinclair, with notes and an introduction by Donald Ferguson. London: Hakluyt Society, 1902 (2nd series, vol. 9). Reprinted, Nendeln, Liechtenstein: Kraus Reprint, 1967. cvii+292p.
An account of Teixeira's travels between Portugal and India during the years 1586-1605, during which time he also visited the Gulf. Qatar is mentioned as a pearl fishery and a port of Arabia, to which the men of Barhen (Bahrain) commonly go to fish. It includes an extensive introduction on Teixeira's life and times.

117 **Arabian sands.**
Wilfred Thesiger. London: Longman, 1959. 326p. 9 maps.
A book recording Thesiger's journeys in Arabia between 1945-51. Qatar is mentioned in connection with Thomas's crossing of Arabia, where he had mapped the well at Dhiby which was 150 miles away from Thesiger's route.

118 **Arabia Felix: across the Empty Quarter of Arabia.**
Bertram Thomas. London: Jonathan Cape, 1932. 397p. 3 maps.
Thomas's account of his crossing of the Rub' al Khali, the first by a European. His journey started at Salala in Dhufar and finished on 5 February 1931 at Doha in Qatar. The book includes appendixes by the author on the regional sands and water-holes, the flora he encountered, a list of camel brands, and a list of Arab chants.

119 **A camel journey across the Rub' al Khali.**
Bertram Thomas. *Geographical Journal*, vol. 78, no. 3 (1931), p. 209-42.
The report of Thomas's 1930-31 first crossing of the Rub' al-Khāli, which finished at Doha. It includes appendixes on the regional sands and water-holes of the Rub' al-Khāli and on the natural history collections gathered on the journey.

120 **Bahrain and the Persian Gulf.**
Maureen Tweedy. Ipswich, England: East Anglian Magazine, 1952. 80p. 3 maps. bibliog.
Qatar is discussed in chapter 4 of this travelogue. It is interesting as a description of the state in the early 1950s, and some aspects of its history are mentioned.

121 **Sons of Sindbad.**
Alan Villiers. London: Hodder & Stoughton, 1940. 346p. 2 maps.
The story of the author's voyages in Arab ships between Basra and Zanzibar. Qatar is briefly mentioned as being surrounded by dangerous waters. The deserted town of Zubara is also noted.

Travel and Exploration

122 A periplus of the Persian Gulf.
Arnold Wilson. *Geographical Journal*, vol. 69, no. 3
(1927), p. 235-59.
A general conspectus of the Gulf. The author's description of Qatar is based on
that of Palgrave.

History of the Arabs from the earliest times to the present.
See item no. 180.

Flora and Fauna

123 **From Oqair to the ruins of Salwa.**
R. E. Cheesman. *Geographical Journal*, vol. 62, no. 5
(Nov. 1923), p. 321-35.
The report of a visit in 1921 by the author, who claims to be the first European
to study the coastline of Arabia between Oqair and Salwa. Qatar is mentioned in
connection with trading routes. The paper is of interest as being an early work to
describe the ornithology of the area.

124 **Handbook of the birds of Europe, the Middle East and North
Africa: the birds of the western Palearctic. Volume 1: ostrich
to ducks.**
Chief editor Stanley Cramp. Oxford, London, New York:
Oxford University Press, 1977. 722p. 175 maps. bibliog.
Provides information on field characteristics, habitat, distribution, population,
movements, food, social patterns and behaviour, voice, breeding, plumages,
moults, and measurements of birds in the western Palaearctic. This region only
includes territory as far east as Kuwait. However, the lack of information on the
birds of the Arabian peninsula suggests that this will be a useful introduction to
the avifauna of Qatar.

125 **Handbook of the birds of Europe, the Middle East and North
Africa: the birds of the western Palearctic. Volume 2: hawks
to bustards.**
Chief editor Stanley Cramp. Oxford, London, New York:
Oxford University Press, 1980. 695p. 164 maps. bibliog.
See preceding entry for details.

126 **The Mollusca of the Persian Gulf, Gulf of Oman and Arabian Sea, as evidenced mainly through the collections of Mr. F. W. Townsend, 1893-1900; with descriptions of new species.**
James Cosmo Melvill, Robert Standen. *Proceedings of the Zoological Society of London*, May-Dec. 1901, p. 327-460.
Qatar was not one of the main mollusc collecting areas used by Townsend, but this paper includes a thorough, if early, catalogue of the species to be found in the Gulf.

127 **The Mollusca of the Persian Gulf, Gulf of Oman, and Arabian Sea, as evidenced mainly through the collections of Mr. F. W. Townsend, 1893-1906; with descriptions of new species. Part 2: Pelecypoda.**
James Cosmo Melvill, Robert Standen. *Proceedings of the Zoological Society of London*, May-Dec. 1906, p. 783-848.
A continuation of the previous entry.

Organisms as producers of carbonate sediment and indicators of environment in the southern Persian Gulf.
See item no. 61.

Falconry in Arabia.
See item no. 537.

Prehistory and Archaeology

128 **Arabian Gulf archaeology.**
Geoffrey Bibby. *Kuml*, 1965, p. 133-52.
A summary of the tenth campaign of the Danish Archaeological Expedition in 1964. In Qatar further excavation was undertaken at the Seleucid period site at Ras Uwainat Ali. Several new Stone Age sites were located at Al-Jubaigib. A large tool-making site was found at Umm Taqa south-east of Dukhan, probably belonging to the mesolithic phase.

129 **The excavation of seven burial cairns on the Ras Abaruk peninsula.**
D. G. Buckley. In: *Qatar archaeological report: excavations 1973.* Edited by Beatrice de Cardi. Oxford, England: Oxford University Press, 1978, p. 120-35.
Seven burial cairns were excavated in the Ras Abaruk peninsula. Although much information was gathered about the structure of the cairns it was impossible to date them. The absence of bone in the cairns is probably due to the high acidity of the sandy soil, and they all showed signs of having been disturbed or robbed.

130 **The excavation of two cairns at al-Da'asa.**
D. G. Buckley. In: *Qatar archaeological report: excavations 1973.* Edited by Beatrice de Cardi. Oxford, England: Oxford University Press, 1978, p. 76-79.
Two burial cairns near the temporary coastal settlement of al-Da'asa were excavated. Due to the lack of finds the cairns could not be dated.

29

Prehistory and Archaeology

131 **Archaeological survey of the northern Trucial States.**
Beatrice de Cardi. *East and West*, n.s., vol. 21, pt. 3-4 (1971), p. 225-89.
Qatar is occasionally mentioned in this text on the archaeology of the northern Trucial States. It is recorded that boats from Julfar regularly fished for pearls off Qatar in the Portuguese period.

132 **The British Archaeological Expedition to Qatar 1973-4.**
Beatrice de Cardi. *Antiquity*, no. 191, vol. 48 (1974), p. 196-200.
A short report on the eight excavations and three area surveys undertaken in ten weeks in 1973-74. Finds of Ubaid-type pottery and flint tools are reported from north-west Qatar. Cairns and a building complex dating from the first few centuries AD were excavated in the Ras Abaruk peninsula. A more permanent settlement of a similar date was located in the Umm al-Ma region. A chain of ruined forts and villages dating from the 17th and 18th centuries, stretching from al-Zubarah along the north and north-eastern coasts, was surveyed.

133 **Qatar archaeological report: excavations 1973.**
Edited by Beatrice de Cardi. Oxford, England: Oxford University Press, for the Qatar National Museum, 1978. 218p. 24 maps. bibliog.
This is the first of a series of volumes which the government of Qatar proposes to publish on the history of the region. It includes fifteen articles presenting the results of the work of the British Archaeological Expedition in Qatar between November 1973 and January 1974. It builds on the surveys undertaken by successive Danish expeditions which have worked in the peninsula since 1956, and it concludes with a gazetteer covering 103 archaeological sites in Qatar.

134 **Sandy land of Qatar.**
Francis Celoria. *Geographical Magazine*, vol. 52, no. 6 (March 1980), p. 395.
A brief discussion of archaeology in Qatar, including a review of Beatrice de Cardi's *Qatar archaeological report* (q.v.).

135 **An encampment of the seventeenth to nineteenth centuries on Ras Abaruk, site 5.**
P. S. Garlake. In: *Qatar archaeological report: excavations 1973*. Edited by Beatrice de Cardi. Oxford, England: Oxford University Press, 1978, p. 164-71.
The settlement appears to represent the remains of a tented encampment of about twenty separate units, with the surviving circles of stones having been used to secure the bottoms of tents. Three similar lines of structures are found in shallow wadis a few hundred metres north of the excavated site. The pottery can be dated from between the 17th and 19th centuries AD.

136 **Fieldwork at al-Huwailah, site 23.**
    P. S. Garlake. In: *Qatar archaeological report: excavations
    1973.* Edited by Beatrice de Cardi. Oxford, England: Oxford
    University Press, 1978, p. 172-79.
Al-Huwailah is the ruin of a town of some historic note, including a fort and a
compact group of stone-built foundations of domestic buildings. The middens
revealed much pottery, which can, from historical sources, be dated to the 18th
century.

137 **A fish-curing complex on Ras Abaruk, site 6.**
    P. S. Garlake. In: *Qatar archaeological report: excavations
    1973.* Edited by Beatrice de Cardi. Oxford, England: Oxford
    University Press, 1978, p. 136-46.
A large accumulation of fish bones in association with a main two-roomed building and a number of fireplaces provides evidence of a fish curing complex at Ras
Abaruk. Its isolation and smallness suggest that it must have been dependent on a
larger community elsewhere, access to which was probably by sea. The only
evidence providing a date is a single decorated vessel of buffware, placing the
complex probably in the first millenium AD.

138 **Archaeological investigations in four Arab states.**
    P. V. Glob. *Kuml,* 1959, p. 233-39.
The summary report of the 1959 Danish archaeological investigations in Kuwait,
Bahrain, Qatar and Abu Dhabi. In Qatar the large town area of Murwab in the
west, dating to the middle of the first millenium BC, was further examined.
Burial mounds at Umm al-Ma and a mesolithic settlement at Al-Wusail were
also excavated. Rock carvings west of Al-Wakrah were studied, and ethnographic
investigations among the Na'im and Murra tribes were undertaken.

139 **Prehistoric discoveries in Qatar.**
    P. V. Glob. *Kuml,* 1957, p. 167-78.
A summary of the first major archaeological survey of the whole of Qatar undertaken in 1957, following the reconnaissance of 1956. Eleven main sites were
discovered, and these were mainly on the coast. Most of them produced few
artefacts, making dating difficult. A large mesolithic settlement was discovered at
Al-Wusail, and a cemetery including fifty cairns was found just to the east of
Umm al-Ma. Several rock carvings south of Al-Furaihah were also studied. The
evidence suggests that settlement in Qatar has covered a period of at least 50,000
years.

140 **Reconnaissance in Qatar.**
    P. V. Glob. *Kuml,* 1956, p. 199-202.
The report of an archaeological reconnaissance of Qatar undertaken in March
1956. Stone cairn grave-mounds were noted at Al-Rufaigh, and Old Stone Age
artefacts were found inland from Ras Uwainat Ali suggesting two settlement
sites.

Prehistory and Archaeology

141 **Atlas of the Stone-Age cultures of Qatar.**
Holger Kapel. Aarhus, Denmark: Aarhus University Press,
1967. [85]p. (Reports of the Danish Archaeological
Expedition to the Arabian Gulf, vol. 1; Jutland
Archaeological Society Publications, vol. 6).
A detailed and comprehensive coverage of the findings of the Danish Archaeological Expedition to Qatar.

142 **Stone Age discoveries in Qatar.**
Holger Kapel. *Kuml*, 1964, p. 112-55.
An evaluation of the eight years of work undertaken by the Danish Archaeological Expedition in Qatar, during which time approximately 200 prehistoric sites were discovered. Of these 141 can be classified as Stone Age sites, and the majority are on the surface. The paper presents a preliminary description and guide to the findings. Four cultural groups are identified: group A - palaeolithic character (30 sites); group B - mesolithic blade-arrowhead culture (8 sites); group C - mesolithic scraper culture (19 sites); group D - neolithic (?) tanged-arrowhead culture (11 sites).

143 **The Arabian peninsula and prehistoric populations.**
Harold A. McClure. Miami, Florida: Field Research
Projects, 1971. 92p. 3 maps. bibliog.
This outlines the palaeoclimatology, palaeogeography and prehistory of Arabia, and notes the flint tool sites discovered in Qatar.

144 **A flint site in Qatar.**
Hans Jørgen Madsen. *Kuml*, 1961, p. 185-201.
A summary of the findings of the 1960 Danish Archaeological Expedition to the west coast of Qatar in which the largest Stone Age find of the Arabian peninsula (by 1960) was discovered.

145 **Prehistory in northeastern Arabia.**
John Oates. *Antiquity*, no. 197, vol. 50 (1976), p. 20-31.
This paper, principally on Saudi Arabia, mentions the sites of al Da'asa and Ras Abaruk in Qatar, as well as the extensive work undertaken there by the Danish Archaeological Expedition.

146 **'Ubaid Mesopotamia and its relation to Gulf countries.**
John Oates. In: *Qatar archaeological report: excavations
1973.* Edited by Beatrice de Cardi. Oxford, England: Oxford
University Press, 1978, p. 39-52.
Al 'Ubaid painted pottery has been found in Qatar at al-Da'asa and Ras Abaruk, and in surface material at Bir Zekrit. This suggests that people in contact with Sumer, in the region of the Euphrates, from where this style of pottery originated, were travelling along the Gulf coast in the 5th millenium BC. This paper also includes a note on the analytical studies undertaken on the prehistoric pottery of Qatar.

Prehistory and Archaeology

147 **Qatar: special presentation by the government of Qatar on the occasion of the inauguration of the Qatar National Museum.**
Newsweek, vol. 85, no. 25 (23 June 1975), 8p.
This provides detailed information on, and photographs of, Qatar's National Museum and its collections of archaeological material, in addition to background information on the state's economy.

148 **National Museum of Qatar, Doha.**
Michael Rice. *Museum* (France), vol. 29, no. 2-3 (1977), p. 78-87.
This paper provides information on the planning behind the creation of Doha's National Museum, and also gives details of the museum's collections and facilities.

149 **The status of archaeology in eastern Arabia and the Arabian Gulf.**
Michael Rice. *Asian Affairs*, vol. 8 (old series vol. 64), no. 2 (1977), p. 139-51.
This survey of Arabian archaeology notes that Qatar is rich in evidence of the Arabian Stone Age. The most remarkable find, according to the author, consists of the designs carved in two rock hills near the north coast at Fuweirat and Jessessiyeh.

150 **Al-Da'asa, site 46: an Arabian neolithic camp site of the fifth millenium.**
G. H. Smith. In: *Qatar archaeological report: excavations 1973.* Edited by Beatrice de Cardi. Oxford, England: Oxford University Press, 1978, p. 53-75.
Evidence from the remains of hearths, domestic tools, pottery of the 'Ubaid cultural type and waste flint indicates the existence of a small temporary encampment at al-Da'asa, which was perhaps visited seasonally during fishing or hunting expeditions. Dates from the late 'Ubaid (3 and 4) pottery suggest that the site was used in the late 5th or early 4th millenium BC. A catalogue by John Oates of the illustrated pottery is included.

151 **Flint tools from Bir Hussein, site 7.**
G. H. Smith. In: *Qatar archaeological report: excavations 1973.* Edited by Beatrice de Cardi. Oxford, England: Oxford University Press, 1978, p. 117-19.
Several crude tools and utilized natural flakes were collected close to an oasis among scattered natural flint flakes. The tools do not fall into any known classification and appear to represent a late degenerate tradition of stone-using.

Prehistory and Archaeology

152 **The stone industries of Qatar.**
G. H. Smith. In: *Qatar archaeological report: excavations 1973.* Edited by Beatrice de Cardi. Oxford, England: Oxford University Press, 1978, p. 35-38.
A refinement of Kapel's classification of four main groups of stone industries in Qatar. It argues that Kapel's C-group should in places be included with the D-group, and that certain differences in the stone assemblages of the D-group suggest a chronological division.

153 **Stone tools from Bir Zekrit, site 50.**
G. H. Smith. In: *Qatar archaeological report: excavations 1973.* Edited by Beatrice de Cardi. Oxford, England: Oxford University Press, 1978, p. 107-16.
Simple flint cutters, scrapers and awls were found on the edge of the oasis at Bir Zekrit. They appear to be of a slightly later date and different tradition of stone-working than at al-Da'asa 46 and Ras Abaruk 4b.

154 **Test excavations in the oasis of Bir Abaruk, site 3.**
G. H. Smith. In: *Qatar archaeological report: excavations 1973.* Edited by Beatrice de Cardi. Oxford, England: Oxford University Press, 1978, p. 26-34.
Three levels of archaeological material were found stratified in silts below the present oasis floor. The upper level contained pottery of probable 17th-20th century date. The middle level yielded pottery of the Barbar period (c. 2,500-2,000 BC). The lowest level included waste flakes and scrapers of neolithic date (c. 4,000 BC).

155 **Two prehistoric sites on Ras Abaruk, site 4.**
G. H. Smith. In: *Qatar archaeological report: excavations 1973.* Edited by Beatrice de Cardi. Oxford, England: Oxford University Press, 1978, p. 80-106.
The settlement area of Ras Abaruk 4 has a large ash midden and a number of spreads of rubble, cairns and ring-walls. One of these ring-wall structures was shown to be a grave pit, surrounded by a wall, which was left open to silt in naturally, thus preventing its dating. The main site can be dated to the neolithic period, but a few sherds were found which possibly date from the late first millenium BC. A catalogue by John Oates of pottery and a report by C. P. Nuttall on the molluscs are also included.

156 **Some data for the study of prehistoric cultural areas on the Persian Gulf.**
Maurizio Tosi. *Proceedings of the [seventh] Seminar for Arabian Studies* (Middle East Centre, Cambridge, England), vol. 4 (1974), p. 145-71.
This paper particularly provides information on middle palaeolithic sites in Qatar.

From Oqair to the ruins of Salwa.
See item no. 123.

History

157 The United Arab Emirates: a modern history.
Muhammad Morsy Abdullah. London: Croom Helm; New
York: Barnes & Noble, 1978. 365p. 8 maps. bibliog.
A detailed, mainly political, study of the development of the United Arab Emirates
as a federal state. There are frequent mentions of Qatar in connection with
the establishment of land and maritime boundaries, and in particular concerning
the Ottoman dispute over al-'Udaid, 1871-1913, and the islands between Abu
Dhabi and Qatar which were finally allocated in the 1969 treaty. Attention is
also paid to the role played by Qatar in the development of education since 1954.

**158 History of eastern Arabia 1750-1800: the rise and
development of Bahrain and Kuwait.**
Ahmad Mustafa Abu Hakima. Beirut: Khayat, 1965. 213p.
5 maps. bibliog.
A consideration of the 'Utbī states in eastern Arabia in the second half of the
18th century. Zubāra in Qatar was established by the 'Utūb in 1766. Chapter 5
considers the Wahhābīs in eastern Arabia and notes the 1787 raid on Qatar by
Sulaymān b. 'Ufayṣān, the Wahhābī general. In the 1790s Zubāra was used as a
shelter for refugees fleeing from the Wahhābī occupation and thus came under
heavy Wahhābī attack. The citadel fell and the 'Utūb inhabitants then migrated
to Bahrain. The 'Utūb are considered to have been important traders in the Gulf
during the 18th century.

159 Qatar: a story of state building.
Ibrahim Abu Nab. [Qatar], 1977. 137p.
A study of the historical evolution of Qatar. It begins with a summary of the life
of the Amir His Highness Sheikh Khalifa Ben Hamad Al-Thani. This is followed
by details of important events in Qatar's history, a survey of the Al-Thani family,
and the development of the oil industry. It concludes with a chapter on the
prospects for the future.

History

160 **Arabia unified: a portrait of Ibn Saud.**
Mohammed Almana. London: Hutchinson Benham, 1980.
328p. 3 maps.
A study of the life and times of Ibn Saud, concentrating particularly on the
period 1925-35 when the author was a translator at the king's court and accompanied him on his expeditions. Qatar is mentioned briefly as the place to which
Prince Abdul Aziz and the Saud family went after taking refuge in Bahrain,
having fled from Riyadh in 1890. It is also noted as the dividing point between
British and American oil interests in the Gulf.

161 **British interests in the Persian Gulf.**
Abdul Amir Amin. Leiden, the Netherlands: E. J. Brill,
1967. 163p. map. bibliog.
An analysis of the reasons for, and the influences of, British intervention in the
Gulf between 1747-78. British settlements during this period were located at
Bandar 'Abbās, Baṣra, and Abū Shahr. British actions in the region were largely
the result of the situation in India and developments in Persia after the death of
Nādir Shah.

162 **The pirate coast.**
Charles Belgrave. Beirut: Librairie du Liban, 1960. 200p.
bibliog.
An account of the Gulf based on the diary of Francis Erskine Loch, written
between 1818-20 when he had the naval command in the Persian Gulf. Qatar is
mainly mentioned in connection with the 1783 raid by Shaikh Ahmed bin Khalifah from Zubara on the Qatar coast against Bahrain, in which he expelled the
Persians. Loch's diary itself did not mention Qatar.

163 **Le prodigieux destin du golfe Persique.** (The prodigious
destiny of the Persian Gulf.)
Jean-Jacques Berreby. *Orient* (France), no. 11, vol. 3
(1959), p. 79-89.
A brief survey of the history of the Gulf from the times of Alexander the Great
to the present age of petroleum.

164 **Progrès et évolution des principautés arabes du Golfe.**
(Progress and evolution of the Arab principalities of the
Gulf.)
Jean-Jacques Berreby. *Orient* (France), no. 25, vol. 7
(1963), p. 25-34.
A study of the development of the Arabian Gulf emirates, which briefly mentions
Qatar while concentrating mainly on Kuwait and Bahrain.

165 **A British official guide to the Gulf.**
Robin L. Bidwell. *Geographical Journal*, vol. 138, no. 2
(1972), p. 233-35.
This is a review article of Lorimer's gazetteer (q.v.).

166 **Yesterday and tomorrow in the Persian Gulf.**

William Brewer. *Middle East Journal*, vol. 23, no. 2 (spring 1969), p. 149-58.

A broad summary of the history of the Gulf, paying particular attention to the role of the British, and the prospects for the area after the announcement on 16 January 1968 that British troops would be withdrawn from the Gulf by the end of 1971. Shaikh Ahmad of Qatar's draft plan addressed to the 25-27 February 1968 meeting of Trucial States' rulers in Dubai is mentioned. The meeting in Doha of the Provisional Council of the Federation of Arab Amirates in September 1968 is also discussed.

167 **Britain and the Gulf - don't go just yet please!: the wisdom of withdrawal reconsidered.**

Neville Brown. *New Middle East*, no. 24 (Sept. 1970), p. 43-46.

An evaluation of the political future of the Gulf following the announcement of 16 January 1968 that Britain would withdraw from the area by the end of 1971. In March 1968 the Federation of the Emirates including Bahrain, Qatar and the seven Trucial States was formed, and it is suggested that this federation was extremely unstable. It is also suggested that if Bahrain seceded Qatar would be liable to do so as well: a prediction that later turned out to be true.

168 **Bahraini strategy for prosperity.**

Denys Brunsden. *Geographical Magazine*, vol. 52, no. 5 (Feb. 1980), p. 349-55.

Qatar is discussed with respect to its historical ties with Bahrain, and the need for current economic unity in the Gulf.

169 **Britain and the Middle East.**

Reader Bullard. London: Hutchinson's University Library, 1951. 3rd rev. ed., 1964. 200p. 2 maps. bibliog.

A general historical introduction to the relations between Britain and the Middle East. Qatar is mentioned as being one of the states which Ibn Saud recognized as being in special treaty relations with Britain. The significance of oil exploitation after the Second World War is also noted.

170 **Britain and the Persian Gulf, 1894-1914.**

Briton Cooper Busch. Berkeley and Los Angeles: University of California Press, 1967. 432p. 6 maps. bibliog.

This book is concerned primarily with the reactions of Britain to what it considered were the aims and interests of other international powers in the Gulf in the two decades before the First World War. Qatar is discussed mainly in connection with the Anglo-Ottoman conflicts there and in neighbouring Bahrain and Kuwait. In the 19th century there was a Turkish garrison at Doha, but Britain also laid claim to Qatar through the 1853 Perpetual Treaty with Bahrain, whose jurisdiction over Qatar was recognized at that time by the British. The British reaction to Turkish expansionism in Qatar in the 1890s is discussed in chapters 5 and 10. Turkey did not abandon its claims to Qatar until 1913, and it was not until 1916 that Britain came to a treaty with Qatar similar to those which it had with the Trucial Coast shaikhdoms. There are eight appendixes giving details of trade and the British officers associated with the Gulf in this period.

171 **Britain, India and the Arabs, 1914-1921.**
Briton Cooper Busch. Berkeley, California: University of California Press, 1971. 522p. 5 maps. bibliog.

An analysis of international relations in the Middle East in the era of the First World War, paying particular attention to the conflict between the British authorities in London and in India. Qatar is discussed on p. 230-31 in connection with the Anglo-Ottoman dispute, and the 1916 treaty with Britain.

172 **Persia and the Persian Question.**
George N. Curzon. London: Longmans, Green & Co., 1892. 2 vols. 10 maps.

A description and analysis of what was known in Britain as 'the Persian Question' at the end of the 19th century. El Katr (Qatar) is mentioned (p. 452-54) in the context of Anglo-Turkish rivalry in the Gulf, and the shaikh at that time, Jasim bin Mohammed bin Thani, is described as 'a mischievous and disorderly character' who 'is quite ready to coquet with any power that will forward his ambitious aims'. This epithet no doubt derived from the shaikh's overtures to the Turks against whom Britain was skirmishing.

173 **The Persian Gulf.**
G. Dalyell. *Scottish Geographical Magazine*, vol. 57, no. 2 (1941), p. 58-65.

A summary of the history of British involvement in the Gulf by the late Political Agent in Bahrain. Doha and Khor al 'Odaid are mentioned in passing, and some information is provided on the early oil concession.

174 **The Bahrein islands (750-1951): a contribution to the study of power politics in the Persian Gulf.**
Abbas Faroughy. New York: Verry, Fisher & Co., 1951. 128p. map. bibliog.

Within this general description and history of Bahrein the close relationship it possessed with Qatar is made clear. In ancient times the name 'Bahrein' was applied to a much larger area, which included mainland Qatar. The book mentions the piracy of Muhammad Ibn Abdallah who fled to Qatar after being forced from Bahrein by the British in 1868. Turkish-British conflict over Qatar in the last quarter of the 19th century is recorded. Article 2 of the Anglo-Turkish Convention of 29 July 1913 stated that Turkey would renounce sovereignty over Qatar, which was to be ruled as in the past by the Sheik Qasim ibn Thani and his successors. The British government also declared that it would not permit the Sheik of Bahrein to interfere with the internal affairs of Qatar.

175 **A description of the Persian Gulf in 1756.**
W. M. Floor. *Persica*, vol. 8 (1979), p. 163-86.

Qatar is not specifically mentioned in this translation of a report written by Tido von Kniphausen and Jan van der Hulst in 1756, but the authors comment that pearl banks reached from Bahrein to Cape Mou-sand (Musandam), thus including Qatar.

176 Gun-running in the Persian Gulf.

Lovet Fraser. *Proceedings of the Central Asian Society*, 17 May 1911, p. 1-16.

An account of gun-running, particularly relating to Bushire and Muscat, during the late 19th and early 20th centuries. It provides a contemporary picture of the background to increased British involvement in the Gulf.

177 The Persian Gulf submarine telegraph of 1864.

C. P. Harris. *Geographical Journal*, vol. 135, no. 2 (1969), p. 169-90.

The story of the creation of the telegraph link between India and Great Britain through the Gulf. Qatar lay within Class 5 of Lieutenant-Colonel Lewis Pelly's jurisdictional classification of 1863.

178 The Trucial States.

Donald Hawley. London: George Allen & Unwin, 1970. 379p. 5 maps. bibliog.

An essentially historical treatment of the Trucial Coast before the British withdrawal in 1971. It discusses the tribal structure of the region in some detail, and provides a diplomatic assessment of the relationships between British officials and the various independent shaikhs in the area during the 19th and 20th centuries. Although mainly concerned with the shaikhdoms now within the United Arab Emirates, it includes many references to Qatar.

179 The Persian Gulf states.

Rupert Hay. Washington, DC: Middle East Institute, 1959. 160p.

An introduction to the geography and history of the Gulf. Qatar is discussed in chapter 10, where the changes to the traditional economy of fishing and pearling brought about by the discovery of oil are noted. The author comments that 'Qatar has few attractions for the visitor from the West other than the possibility of doing business'.

180 History of the Arabs from the earliest times to the present.

Philip K. Hitti. London: Macmillan, 1970. 10th ed. 822p. 21 maps.

In this general history of the Arabs Qatar is mentioned as being an autonomous shaikhdom dependent on Britain. This relationship was regulated by the 1916 treaty. Qatar is also mentioned in connection with Thomas's crossing of the al-Rab' al-Khāli.

181 Arabia.

David George Hogarth. Oxford, England: Clarendon Press, 1922. 139p.

A short history of Arabia. In the period under discussion the area later to be known as Qatar is referred to as mainland Bahrain.

History

182 Farewell to Arabia.

David Holden. London: Faber & Faber, 1966. 268p. 3 maps. bibliog.

This is, according to the author, 'an attempt to picture the process of change in action', as Arabia underwent 'revolutionary' changes during the 1950s and 1960s. Qatar is mentioned mostly in chapters 10, 11 and 12 in connection with the role of the British in the Gulf. The beginnings of oil exploitation are discussed, alongside the border conflicts between Qatar and its neighbours Bahrain and Saudi Arabia. The main theme of the book concerns the manner in which different parts of the Arabian peninsula have thrown off their old characteristics, often with violence as in Yemen, and become 'part of the common consciousness of the world'.

183 Background of the British position in Arabia.

Halford Lancaster Hoskins. *Middle East Journal*, vol. 1, no. 2 (1947), p. 137-47.

This paper briefly analyses the history of Britain's relationship with Arabia.

184 British routes to India.

Halford Lancaster Hoskins. London: Frank Cass, 1928. New ed., 1966. 494p. map.

An account of British attempts to ensure safe and relatively quick routes to India in the 18th and 19th centuries. The Persian Gulf receives scattered mentions.

185 Reminiscences of the map of Arabia and the Persian Gulf.

F. Fraser Hunter. *Geographical Journal*, vol. 54, no. 6 (1919), p. 355-63.

A paper on the construction of the maps made to accompany Lorimer's gazetteer (q.v.) which were compiled by the author of this article. The murder of the shaikh of Qatar in 1906, following a quarrel with the shaikh of Bahrain over a pearl, is mentioned.

186 The Gulf: Arabia's western approaches.

Molly Izzard. London: John Murray, 1979. 314p. map. bibliog.

A study of the political and economic history of the Gulf, which is mixed with the author's personal experiences of the region. Qatar is described in chapter 16.

187 Arabia, the Gulf and the West.

John B. Kelly. London: Weidenfeld & Nicholson, 1980. 530p. 5 maps. bibliog.

The author argues that despite a gloss of recently acquired modernity the Gulf today is still much as it always has been, and that the resultant instability poses a major threat to Western interests in the region. Qatar is discussed in detail between p. 185-93. Its early history of occupation by the Al Khalifah rulers of Bahrain, who migrated from Kuwait to Zubara in 1766, followed by the Al Thani attempts to throw off their tribute, is mentioned. The acknowledgement in 1871 of Turkish suzerainty by Jasim, the son of Shaikh Muhammad ibn Thani, led to the eventual cessation of this tribute paid to Bahrain. Qatar was brought into the

British trucial system through the 1916 treaty, and the first oil concession was granted in 1935. The subsequent discovery and exploitation of oil are seen as having materially transformed the society, and the problems of Asian immigrant labour, particularly from Pakistan, are also noted. At present the Al Thani are seen as being by far the dominant tribe, but uncertainty as to the likely maintenance of this strict control is expressed. This useful book also includes details of boundary agreements and relations with the other neighbouring states of the Arabian peninsula.

188 Britain and the Persian Gulf, 1795-1880.

John B. Kelly. Oxford, England: Oxford University Press, 1968. 911p. 2 maps. bibliog.

The most complete account of Britain's relationship with the Gulf in the 19th century, which was maintained through her control of the sea. There are numerous mentions of Qatar, particularly in connection with the rise of the Wahhabis, Turkish suzerainty of the peninsula, piracy, and the Al Khalifah possessions in Qatar. A general description of Qatar at this period is found at the beginning of the book (p. 25-28).

189 The legal and historical basis of the British position in the Persian Gulf.

John B. Kelly. In: *St. Antony's Papers, vol. 4.* London: Oxford University Press, 1958, p. 119-40.

A study concentrating on the legacy of the past in its effects on British policy in the Gulf. The vague status of Qatar in the mid-19th century is noted. In 1867 Shaikh Muhammad ibn Khalifah of Bahrain made a savage attack on Dauhah and Wakrah to punish them for insubordination, and as a result of British intervention Qatar was brought, to a certain extent, into the trucial system. The Saudi Amir, Faisal ibn Turki, also laid claim to the peninsula. The assertion of Turkish jurisdiction over the west of the Gulf as far as Qatar caused considerable problems for the British. It is argued that British concern with maritime truces rather than an involvement on the land was significant for later developments.

190 Anglo-Turkish antagonism in the Persian Gulf.

Ravinder Kumar. *Islamic Culture*, vol. 37, no. 2 (1963), p. 100-11.

This paper on the British and Ottoman attempts to gain superiority in the Gulf in the 19th century describes the 1871 Ottoman expedition to Arabia which sent an emissary to Qatar to persuade the ruler to accept Ottoman suzerainty. The British argued that Qatar was bound by the agreements on maritime peace that had been negotiated with Bahrain in 1868.

191 India and the Persian Gulf region, 1858-1907: a study in British imperial policy.

Ravinder Kumar. London: Asia Publishing House, 1965. 259p. bibliog.

The Gulf is identified as a cockpit of international rivalry in the 19th century. The confrontation between the British and Turkish governments over Qatar is mentioned in some detail.

History

192 **Gulf states.**
Robert G. Landen. In: *The Middle East: its governments and politics.* Edited by Abid A. Al-Marayati. Belmont, California: Duxbury Press, 1972, p. 295-316.

Provides an account of the historical background, economic and social environment, political structure, political processes, oil related problems, foreign policy and political prospects of the Gulf states. The foundation of the short-lived pearl-fishing city-state of Zubarah in Qatar in the 1760s, Qatar's independence in 1971, the state's oil developments, Qatar's legal apparatus, and its political allegiances are all mentioned.

193 **Gazetteer of the Persian Gulf, 'Omān, and central Arabia.**
J. G. Lorimer. Calcutta, India: Government Printing House, 1908-15. 2 vols. Reprinted, Farnborough, England: Gregg International; Dublin: Irish University Press, 1970.

Useful as an introduction to British interests in the peninsula in the 19th and early 20th centuries. Qatar is specifically discussed in vol. 2, p. 1,505-35. Burchardt is referred to as the only European to have visited the interior of Qatar before the publication of the gazetteer. Much of the article on Qatar is occupied by a list of the chief places, bays, headlands, hills and islands forming the coast. The fact that nearly all of the desert wells were masonry-lined is noted as a remarkable peculiarity of Qatar. Pearl fishing and the breeding of camels are noted as the main sources of income.

194 **Britain and the Persian Gulf: mistaken timing over Aden.**
William Luce. *Round Table,* no. 227 (July 1967), p. 277-83.

A study of the factors behind Britain's continued presence in the Gulf despite her withdrawal from India, set against the contradictory forces tending towards unity and disunity between nations in the area.

195 **The Persian Gulf.**
H. F. B. Lynch. *Imperial Asiatic Quarterly Review,* 3rd series, vol. 13 (April 1902), p. 225-34.

An article investigating German, Turkish and Russian attempts to violate the supremacy of the British in the Gulf at the turn of the 20th century.

196 **America and the Arabian peninsula: the first two hundred years.**
Joseph J. Malone. *Middle East Journal,* vol. 30 (1976), p. 406-24.

An investigation into the rapid expansion of the American presence in Arabia, from its first conflicts with Britain to its involvement in the oil industry. There was no early American Arabian Mission in Qatar as there were in neighbouring Kuwait and Bahrain. Mention is made of Sarah Hosman's missionary tour to Hasa, Qatar and the Trucial Oman in the 1920s. Much emphasis is paid to the British and American conflicts of interest over oil exploration.

197 The Middle East: a political and economic survey.
Edited by Peter Mansfield. London, New York: Oxford
University Press, 1950. 4th ed., 1973. 591p. 3 maps. bibliog.
Qatar is analysed on p. 195-97 of the chapter on Arabia in this survey of the
Middle East. It mentions the 1972 bloodless *coup* in which Shaikh Ahmad ibn
Ali al-Thani was ousted by his cousin Shaikh Khalifa ibn Hamad al-Thani, who
was then deputy ruler, heir to the throne, and prime minister. Qatar's 1916
agreement with Britain, the conflicts with Bahrain and the development of the oil
industry are all discussed.

198 The Persian Gulf in the twentieth century.
John Marlowe. London: Cresset Press, 1962. 278p. 2 maps.
bibliog.
Qatar is described in this general introduction to the Gulf as having little
independent history of any importance. Details of the 1916 agreement making
Qatar, to all intents and purposes, a British protectorate are given, as is information relating to the concession obtained by the Anglo-Persian Oil Company on
behalf of IPC (Iraq Petroleum Company) in 1935. Most of the other references
to Qatar are related to the expansion of the oil industry. The abdication of
Sheikh Ali in 1959, arranged by the Chief Political Resident Persian Gulf and
marked by the arrival of a British gunboat off Doha, is also mentioned.

199 The countries and tribes of the Persian Gulf.
S. B. Miles. London: Harrison & Sons, 1919. 2 vols.
Al-Katar (Qatar) is mentioned briefly in connection with pearl fishing in this
book based on the notes made by Colonel Miles during his time spent around the
Persian Gulf in the second half of the 19th century.

200 Britain's moment in the Middle East 1914-1956.
Elizabeth Monroe. London: Chatto & Windus, 1963. 254p.
2 maps. bibliog.
A survey of the means by which Britain was able to maintain supremacy in the
Middle East for forty years. Qatar is mentioned as being on one of the major
oilfields of the region, which by chance lay on the route to India which Britain
had sought to protect, and as being one of a number of 'family estates' which
consequently became British protectorates.

201 The pirates of the Trucial Oman.
H. Moyse-Bartlett. London: Macdonald, 1966. 256p. 5
maps. bibliog.
Although this book provides little direct information concerning Qatar it nevertheless supplies an interesting account of the 19th century relationship between the
British and the inhabitants of the lower Gulf, particularly concerning the piratical
activities of the Qawasim.

History

202 The Ottoman Turks and the Portuguese in the Persian Gulf, 1534-1581.
Salih Özbaran. *Journal of Asian History*, vol. 6, no. 1 (1972), p. 45-87.
A detailed account of Portuguese and Turkish involvement in the Gulf, paying particular attention to Bahrayn, Basra and Hormuz. Qatar is mentioned in connection with the struggle between Portugal and the Ottomans for the island of Bahrayn. The appendixes include a number of interesting letters between government officials in the 16th century.

203 British policy towards the Arabian tribes on the shores of the Persian Gulf (1864-1868).
Dharm Pal. *Journal of Indian History*, vol. 24 (1945), p. 60-76.
This paper argues that British policy towards the Gulf tribes was governed mainly by trade interests. It is concerned with the period following the appointment of Lieutenant-Colonel Lewis Pelly as Political Resident of the Persian Gulf territories. It notes the attack on Guttar (Qatar) by men belonging to the chiefs of Bahrein and Aboothabee (Abu Dhabi) in October 1867, which the British were powerless to stop. The Guttar tribes retaliated on Bahrein in June 1868 and the author notes that in the ensuing sea battle some 600 craft were destroyed with upwards of 1,000 lives lost.

204 Remarks on the pearl oyster beds in the Persian Gulf.
Lewis Pelly. *Transactions of the Bombay Geographical Society*, vol. 18 (Jan. 1865-Dec. 1867), p. 32-36.
A brief report on pearling in the mid-19th century, by the British Political Resident in the Persian Gulf. Most attention is given to Bahrein.

205 Remarks on the tribes, trade, and resources around the shore line of the Persian Gulf.
Lewis Pelly. *Transactions of the Bombay Geographical Society*, vol. 17 (Jan. 1863-Dec. 1864), p. 32-112.
A collection of what the author calls superficial remarks based on personal observation and hearsay concerning the Gulf. Qatar is classified in the author's fifth category of territories, as being held by an independent maritime Arab chief bound by the terms of a permanent truce to keep the peace at sea, with the English Resident in the Gulf being mediator and quasi-guarantee for the observation of this truce. Paragraph 107 notes that Gutter (Qatar) was a subject district of Bahrein, and pearling is seen as the mainstay of its economy.

206 Arabia.
H. St. John B. Philby. London: Ernest Benn, 1930. 387p.
A history of Arabia concentrating on the period since AD 1703, the year of Muhammad Ibn 'Abdul Wahhab's birth. Eighteenth century raids against Qatar by the Wahhabis, the 1783 annexation of Bahrain by the 'Atban (Utub) Arabs from their colony at Zubara on the Qatar peninsula, 'Abdul Rahman's 1891 flight from Riyadh during which he paused at Qatar, and Ibn Saud's interference in the dispute between Qasim ibn Thani and his brother Ahmad in Qatar in 1905 are all mentioned.

207 **Wahhabism and Saudi Arabia.**
George Rentz. In: *The Arabian peninsula: society and politics.* Edited by Derek Hopwood. London: George Allen & Unwin, 1972, p. 54-66.
An analysis of the development of the Wahhabi state. Qatar is mentioned with reference to the two expeditions from Najd which reached its coasts in the 1780s.

208 **Bahrain: social and political change since the First World War.**
M. G. Rumaihi. Epping, England: Bowker, with the Centre for Middle Eastern and Islamic Studies of the University of Durham, 1976. 258p. bibliog.
This detailed account of development in Bahrain mentions Qatar in connection with the relations between Britain and Turkey in the region in the late 19th century.

209 **The Arabian peninsula.**
Richard Sanger. Ithaca, New York: Cornell University Press, 1954. 295p. 2 maps. bibliog.
An analysis of the growing influence of the West on Arabia, and in particular the role of the USA in 'developing' the region. Qatar is seen as being a particularly inhospitable country, which, if it were not for the discovery of the Dukhan oil-field, would probably only be inhabited by a small number of bedouin. Bertram Thomas's crossing of the Empty Quarter which finished at Doha is also mentioned.

210 **Historical sketch of the Gulf in the Islamic era from the seventh to the eighteenth century A.D.**
R. B. Serjeant. In: *Qatar archaeological report: excavations 1973.* Edited by Beatrice de Cardi. Oxford, England: Oxford University Press, 1978, p. 147-63.
A useful summary of the history of Qatar within the broader area of the Gulf before 1800. It covers details of the political structure, civilization and trade during the 'Abbasid era, the role of the Portuguese in the Gulf during the early 16th century, and the mercantile activities of the British and the Dutch in the 17th century.

211 **Pirates or polities? Arab societies of the Persian or Arabian Gulf, 18th century.**
Louise E. Sweet. *Ethnohistory*, vol. 11 (1964), p. 262-80.
An analysis of the nature and potential scale of integration of Arab societies in the Gulf in the period 1750-1820. Mention is made of the 'Utub alliance dominating Kuwait, Bahrain and Qatar, which was in opposition to the Jowasim of the Trucial States. It argues that the Sunni Arab seafaring lineages were a controlling élite class or caste in coastally focused polities and settlements with mixed ethnic or sectarian populations.

History

212 The Persian Gulf.
Compiled and edited by R. Hughes Thomas. Bombay, India: Bombay Education Society's Press, for the government, 1856. 687p. 6 maps. (Selections from the Records of the Bombay Government, n.s., no. 24).

Provides a wide range of information on the provinces of Oman, Muscat, Bahrain and other places in the Gulf, including details of treaties, tables of events, navigation, the suppression of the slave trade, and tribal activities. Mention is made of Al Bidder town in connection with pearling; Biddah; Wukrah, noted as recently constructed; Khor Hassan, a town of 400 houses, being the former retreat of Shaikh Rahman bin Jabir Yalahimi; and Zobara, another town of 400 houses. All of these settlements lie in what is now Qatar, but Qatar as such is not mentioned. Khor Hassan and Zobara are noted as belonging to Bahrain.

213 Arab navigation in the Indian Ocean before the coming of the Portuguese, being a translation of 'Kitāb al-fawā'id fī uṣūl al-baḥr wa 'l-qawā'id' of Aḥmad b. Mājid al-Najdi, together with an introduction on the history of Arab navigation.
G. R. Tibbetts. London: Royal Asiatic Society of Great Britain and Ireland, 1971. 614p. 7 maps. bibliog. (Oriental Translation Fund, n.s., vol. 42).

A translation of ibn Mājid's Fawā'id which was written c. 1489-90, together with an extensive introduction to Arab navigation. It notes that, except for a short poem on navigation in the Persian Gulf, this sea is omitted by all the navigators. Nevertheless Qatar is mentioned in the ninth fā'ida which deals with the coasts of the world.

214 Arabia in the fifteenth century navigational texts.
G. R. Tibbetts. Arabian Studies, vol. 1 (1974), p. 86-101.

Ra's Laffan and al-Ra's in Qatar are noted as coastal bearing points in statistics derived from Arab navigational texts. This paper also mentions that the Portuguese names for Qatar were Catar and Quatara.

215 The records of the British Residency and Agencies in the Persian Gulf.
Penelope Tuson. London: India Office Library and Records, Foreign and Commonwealth Office, 1979. 201p. map. bibliog.

This is an introduction to, and list of, the British India Office Records relating to the Persian Gulf. Although there was not a British Agency in Qatar, affairs relating to the country in the 19th century were supervised by the Resident at Bushire. In 1949 a Political Officer, subordinate to the Political Agent Bahrain, was eventually posted to Doha. Records relating to Qatar include details of boundaries, correspondences, oil, a hospital, and defence measures.

216 **The British withdrawal from the Gulf and its consequences.**
Anthony Verrier. In: *Middle East focus: the Persian Gulf.*
Edited by T. Cuyler Young. Princeton, New Jersey:
Princeton University Conference, 1969, p. 134-49.
An evaluation of the British role in the Gulf, which concludes that the consequences of withdrawal are incalculable. Qatar is mentioned as one of the states which might possibly have formed a federation.

217 **A sketch of the historical geography of the Trucial Oman down to the beginning of the sixteenth century.**
J. C. Wilkinson. *Geographical Journal,* vol. 130, no. 3
(1964), p. 337-49.
Although this paper concentrates on the seven Trucial States there are scattered references to Qatar in connection with pearling, the writings of early Arab authors, and mesolithic and neolithic finds.

218 **The Persian Gulf: an historical sketch from the earliest times to the beginning of the twentieth century.**
Arnold T. Wilson. Oxford, England: Clarendon Press,
1928. 327p. map. bibliog.
This history of the Gulf mentions the 1895 attempt by tribes from Qatar, mainly the Al bin Ali who had settled at Zubara, to invade Bahrain under Turkish influence. This uprising was quelled by British vessels which opened fire and destroyed or captured most of the Qatar boats.

219 **The creation of Qatar.**
Rosemarie Said Zahlan. London: Croom Helm, 1979.
160p. 2 maps. bibliog.
A detailed account of the development of the independent state of Qatar, with a concluding chapter on its future to the year 2000. Much of the emphasis of the book is on the relationship between oil and political activity, from the early oil concessions and treaties with Britain to the use of oil for providing social welfare benefits. A central chapter discusses the territorial disputes with Saudi Arabia and Bahrain from which the modern state emerged. There are three appendixes providing details of the Al-Thani family and the treaties of 1868 and 1916.

220 **Hegemony, dependence and development in the Gulf.**
Rosemarie Said Zahlan. In: *Social and economic development in the Arab Gulf.* Edited by Tim Niblock.
London: Croom Helm, 1980, p. 61-79.
A study of the historical socio-economic context within which strategies and policies must function. It discusses the important role of pearling in the pre-British economy of Qatar, and the oil agreements between Shaikh Abdallah and the British.

History

221 **The origins of the United Arab Emirates. A political and social history of the Trucial States.**
Rosemarie Said Zahlan. London: Macmillan, 1978. 278p. map. bibliog.
Although specifically related to the seven emirates comprising the United Arab Emirates, this thorough and useful book discusses Qatar in connection with the planned federation of Gulf states after the British withdrawal (p. 194-95), the 1935 boundary dispute with Saudi Arabia and Abu Dhabi (p. 136-37), and oil concessions (p. 110-18).

222 **Arabia: the cradle of Islam. Studies in the geography, people and politics of the peninsula with an account of Islam and mission work.**
S. M. Zwemer. New York: Fleming H. Revell, 1900. 2nd rev. ed. 437p. 8 maps. bibliog.
The purpose of this book was to draw attention to Arabia at a time when there was little material published about the peninsula, and in particular to emphasize the need for Christian missionary work among the Arabs. El Katar (Qatar) is described as being unattractive in every way and barren enough to be called a desert (p. 110-11). The author estimates that there were 200 pearling boats operating out of Qatar in the late 19th century, and notes that the whole peninsula is claimed by Turkey.

Qatar and its people.
See item no. 21.

Géographie d'Edrisi. (Edrisi's geography.)
See item no. 65.

The travels of Pedro Teixeira with his 'Kings of Harmuz' and extracts from his 'Kings of Persia'.
See item no. 116.

Bahrain and the Persian Gulf.
See item no. 120.

Bahrain, Qatar, and the United Arab Emirates: colonial past, present problems, and future prospects.
See item no. 287.

Eastern Arabian frontiers.
See item no. 320.

International relations of Arabia: the dependent areas.
See item no. 324.

Indo-Arab relations: an account of India's relations with the Arab world from ancient up to modern times.
See item no. 413.

The past and present connection of England with the Persian Gulf.
See item no. 415.

The Persian Gulf route and commerce.
See item no. 416.

The golden bubble: Arabian Gulf documentary.
See item no. 458.

Arab seafaring in the Indian Ocean in ancient and early medieval times.
See item no. 494.

Population

223 La personalité géographique des villes des émirats du Golfe.
(The geographical personality of the towns of the Gulf emirates.)
André Bourgey. *Maghreb Machrek*, vol. 81 (1978), p. 56-62.

This is essentially concerned with the demography of the main towns of the Gulf emirates. It includes many mentions of Doha.

224 Contemporary urban growth in the Middle East.
John I. Clarke. In: *Change and development in the Middle East: essays in honour of W. B. Fisher.* Edited by John I. Clarke, Howard Bowen-Jones. London, New York: Methuen, 1981, p. 154-70.

This essay notes that Qatar has never had a full census, and that it has no official definition of urban status. It was previously published in *The changing Middle Eastern city* (edited by R. I. Lawless, G. H. Blake. London: Croom Helm, 1980).

225 Populations of the Middle East and North Africa: a geographical approach.
Edited by J. I. Clarke, W. B. Fisher. London: University of London Press, 1972. 432p.

A geographical introduction to the demography of the Middle East. Qatar is mentioned in chapter 11 by A. G. Hill.

226 **L'immigration dans la péninsule arabique.** (Immigration in the Arabian peninsula.)
Nicolas Hemsay. *Maghreb Machrek*, vol. 85 (1979), p. 55-60.

An analysis of the socio-economic effects of the large scale immigration to the peninsula, including Qatar, resulting from the accumulation of petroleum revenue.

227 **The Gulf states: petroleum and population growth.**
A. G. Hill. In: *Populations of the Middle East and North Africa: a geographical approach.* Edited by J. I. Clarke, W. B. Fisher. London: University of London Press, 1972, p. 242-73.

This chapter considers each of the five Arab Gulf states in turn, and Qatar is discussed on p. 262-64. It argues that exact statements concerning Qatar's population were impossible before the results of the 1970 census were published. Mention is made of the 1963 and 1964 laws dealing with immigration, and the first nationality law of 1961.

228 **The population situation in the ECWA region: Qatar.**
Beirut: United Nations Economic Commission for Western Asia, 1980. 26p. map. bibliog.

Provides detailed information on population size, distribution and structure, fertility, mortality, migration, growth rates, education, and population policy in Qatar.

Impact of technical change on the structure of the labour force in the ECWA region.
See item no. 529.

Nationalities and Minorities

229 **Ethnic conflict: a framework of analysis and its relevance to the Gulf region.**
Abdul Aziz Said. In: *Conflict and cooperation in the Persian Gulf*. Edited by Mohammed Mughisuddin. New York, London: Praeger, 1977, p. 103-15.
This paper notes that Qatar is a successor to colonial territory, and that it has a multiplicity of peoples living within it.

The Middle East: a social geography.
See item no. 235.

Arab manpower: the crisis of development.
See item no. 506.

Economic and social implications of current development in the Arab Gulf: the oriental connection.
See item no. 507.

International migration and development in the Arab region.
See item no. 508.

International Migration Project country case study: the State of Qatar.
See item no. 509.

The nature and process of labour importing: the Arabian Gulf states of Kuwait, Bahrain, Qatar and the United Arab Emirates.
See item no. 510.

Some aspects of the labour market in the Middle East, with special reference to the Gulf states.
See item no. 511.

Language

230 **Courtesies in the Gulf area: a dictionary of colloquial phrase and usage.**
Donald Hawley.   London: Stacey International, 1978. 96p. map.

This provides a useful introduction to Arabic phrases used in the Gulf, covering a wide range of topics from greetings and farewells to condolences. It also includes vocabularies and a chapter on Omani proverbs. All phrases are written in Arabic with translations and transliterations.

The Persian Gulf states.
See item no. 9.

Social Conditions

231 **Kuwait and her neighbours.**
   H. R. P. Dickson.   London: George Allen & Unwin, 1956.
   627p. 6 maps.

Personal reminiscences of the author who was Political Agent at Kuwait from 1929-36 and afterwards the chief local representative of the Kuwait Oil Company. The migration of the Al Sabah and Al Khalifah from inner Najd to Zubara on the Qatar peninsula and then to Kuwait in 1710 is mentioned in a section on the early history of the region. A section on tribes notes that the Sharif tribes of the Bani Hajir and the Bani Tamim live in Qatar. There is some mention of Qatar in connection with the rivalry between Britain and Turkey in the 19th century. Other incidental references to Qatar, including mention of its oil discoveries, may be found.

232 **The United Arab Emirates: an economic and social survey.**
   K. G. Fenelon.   London, New York: Longman, 1976. 2nd
   ed. 164p. 3 maps. bibliog.

A general survey of the United Arab Emirates in which several references to Qatar are found in connection with pearling, the early oil concessions (chapter 5), and the British withdrawal.

233 **Class struggle in the Arab Gulf.**
   Fred Halliday.   *New Left Review*, vol. 58 (1969), p. 31-37.

An evaluation of the potential of the Popular Front for the Liberation of the Occupied Arab Gulf based largely on the revolution in Yemen and the Dhofar. It suggests that the attempt by Britain to create a union of Arab emirates on its departure from the Gulf in 1971 was doomed to failure. Qatar is mentioned as one of the nine Arab entities in the Gulf over which Britain had control. It predicts that the PFLOAG will cause great damage to imperialism, and that the 'miserable neo-colonialist plots' Britain was hatching can be defeated.

234 **Social change in the Gulf states and Oman.**
Frauke Heard-Bey. *Asian Affairs*, vol. 59, pt. 3 (1972), p.
309-16.
This paper notes that, due largely to the discovery of oil, foreign immigrants now
outnumber the indigenous inhabitants of Qatar.

235 **The Middle East: a social geography.**
Stephen H. Longrigg. London: Gerald Duckworth, 1963.
2nd rev. ed., 1970. 291p. 4 maps. bibliog.
Qatar is described as being patriarchal, with little external history and with great
wealth derived from oil, in this general account of the different races and social
forces found in the Middle East.

236 **The Arabian peninsula and annotated bibliography.**
Louise E. Sweet. In: *The Central Middle East: a
handbook of anthropology.* Edited by Louise E. Sweet. New
Haven, Connecticut: Human Relations Area Files, 1968, p.
271-355.
Qatar is mentioned briefly as a country where fishing was the predominant sub-
sistence pattern and where oil development has now had an effect.

237 **Center-periphery interaction patterns: the case of Arab visits,
1946-1975.**
W. R. Thompson. *International Organization*, vol. 35, no.
2 (1981), p. 355-73.
Qatar is one of a number of Middle Eastern countries to be used as examples in
a test of a theoretical model of centre-periphery interaction patterns.

238 **Qatar: toward the welfare sheikhdom?**
S. A. Wady-Ramahi. *Mid East*, vol. 8, no. 1 (1968), p.
15-19.
An account of socio-economic changes that have taken place within Qatar consequent on the exploitation of oil. It notes that almost one-third of the national
revenue is apportioned to social services.

239 **Qatar: progressive puritans.**
M. Wall. *The Economist*, vol. 235 (6 June 1970), suppl.,
p. XXII-XXVII.
This note in a special report on the Arabian peninsula observes that Qatar has
the largest and most powerful ruling family of any of the Gulf states, and it
provides some information on Qatar's oil industry.

**Bahrain, Qatar, and the United Arab Emirates: colonial past, present
problems, and future prospects.**
See item no. 287.

Social Conditions

Social and political change in the Third World: some peculiarities of oil-producing principalities of the Persian Gulf.
See item no. 289.

Social and economic development in the Arab Gulf.
See item no. 372.

Problems and prospects of development in the Arabian peninsula.
See item no. 396.

Focus on Qatar.
See item no. 407.

Qatar.
See item no. 427.

Oil, social change and economic development in the Arabian peninsula.
See item no. 476.

Values, social organization and technology change in the Arab world.
See item no. 533.

Social Services, Health and Welfare

240 **Transcultural aspects of psychiatric patients in Qatar.**
M. Fakhr el-Islam. *Comparative Medicine East and West*,
vol. 6, no. 1 (1978), p. 33-36.
This paper discusses the importance of somatic symptoms in determining the
patient role and patient-doctor relationship in the light of cultural characteristics
of the Qatari community. It argues that delusory cultural beliefs related to possession, sorcery and envy provide a conceptual framework for the explanation of
many disorders.

241 **Thalassæmia-Hæmoglobin E disease: a case report from Quatar
(Persian Gulf).**
M. Shahid, G. Abu Haydar, N. Abu Haydar. *Man*, vol. 63
(1963), p. 129-30.
The case of an eight-year-old male born in Doha suffering from Thalassæmia-
Hæmoglobin E disease. This is the first report of the disease from the Gulf area.
It is encountered most frequently in South-east Asia and the authors suggest that
it may have been transplanted by pilgrims or merchants.

Politics

242 1971-1981: a decade of progress.
Daily Gulf Times, 2 Sept. 1981, suppl. 32p.
A report on Qatar's achievements in the ten years since independence in September 1971. It provides information on foreign policy, unity, politics, education, farming, the university, the courts, oil and gas, industry, public health, Gulf Air, and sport.

243 Oil, power and politics: conflict in Arabia, the Red Sea and the Gulf.
Mordechai Abir. London: Frank Cass, 1974. 221p. 3 maps. bibliog.
A selection of papers, mainly concerning the effects of the decline of British power in the region. Qatar is discussed in connection with the establishment of the federation of smaller emirates, which, despite Saudi Arabia's wishes, it did not join.

244 The development of the Gulf states.
Ahmad Mustafa Abu-Hakima. In: *The Arabian peninsula: society and politics.* Edited by Derek Hopwood. London: George Allen & Unwin, 1972, p. 31-53.
A summary of the political structure and development of the Arab Gulf states. Qatar is discussed on p. 44-47 where the struggle of the Al Thani shaikhs to achieve independence from the Al Khalifah's dominance in the 19th century is mentioned. The eclipse of Ottoman authority by Britain and the 1916 treaty between Britain and Qatar are also discussed.

245 Politics in the Gulf.
M. S. Agwani. New Delhi: Vikas Publishing House, 1978. 199p. bibliog.
This book analyses the political conflicts in the Gulf resulting from its importance as an oil producer. Information is provided on the economic and constitutional development of Qatar, and the planned federation of Gulf states at Britain's

departure, which eventually led to the creation of the United Arab Emirates, Bahrain and Qatar. Sea-bed treaties between Qatar and Iran and Abu Dhabi are mentioned on p. 67.

246 **The security of the Persian Gulf.**
Edited by Hossein Amirsadeghi. London: Croom Helm, 1981. 294p. 2 maps. bibliog.
Qatar is mentioned in the papers by John Duke Anthony and Edmund Ghareeb in this book on Gulf security in the wake of the Iranian revolution. The editor believes that the Khomeini régime in Iran will eventually collapse, and argues that if Soviet-backed extremists gain the upper hand the likelihood of an East-West confrontation over the Gulf's energy resources will be greatly increased.

247 **Oil policies of the Gulf countries.**
William D. Anderson. In: *Conflict and cooperation in the Persian Gulf.* Edited by Mohammed Mughisuddin. New York, London: Praeger, 1977, p. 60-78.
This paper on the oil industry notes that the original oil concession in Qatar ran for seventy-five years. It also observes that oil generates more revenue than can be used in Qatar, and that the country generally follows Saudi Arabian policies.

248 **The Persian Gulf as a regional subsystem.**
William D. Anderson. In: *Conflict and cooperation in the Persian Gulf.* Edited by Mohammed Mughisuddin. New York, London: Praeger, 1977, p. 1-12.
Qatar is noted as being one of the countries which the pro-Palestinian terrorists who captured OPEC oil ministers in Vienna in December 1975 identified as being tools of US imperialism.

249 **Arab states of the lower Gulf: people, politics, petroleum.**
John Duke Anthony. Washington, DC: Middle East Institute, 1975. 273p. map. bibliog. (James Terry Duce Memorial Series, vol. 3).
Before a discussion of the individual states of the lower Gulf, this book isolates four general themes: the changing social and demographic structure of the indigenous and immigrant populations; the shifting alliances between and among the rulers of the individual emirates; the clash between traditional and modernizing forces; and the relationships between the shaikhdoms and the states outside the area. Qatar is discussed in chapter 3, where the author argues that the élite structure of the state is comprised essentially of the vast Al Tnani family, and that the export of oil beginning in 1949 has led to great socio-political as well as economic changes. The take-over of the government by Shaikh Khalifa from his cousin Shaikh Ahmad in 1962 is discussed within the framework of the traditional rivalry between the Bani Hamad, Bani 'Ali and Bani Khalid branches of the ruling family.

Politics

250 **The Persian Gulf in regional and international politics: the Arab side of the Gulf.**
John Duke Anthony. In: *The security of the Persian Gulf.* Edited by Hossein Amirsadeghi. London: Croom Helm, 1981, p. 170-96.

An analysis of the local and regional aims of the Arab governments of the Gulf in terms of the nature of political interaction among the states, the contest between conservative and radical régimes in the area, and the connection between these states and the Arab-Israeli conflict. Among territorial disputes in the region that between Bahrain and Qatar over the Hawar Islands is noted as being of importance. Mention is made of the Arab Military Industries Organization of which Qatar is a member, alongside Saudi Arabia, the United Arab Emirates and Egypt. It is also noted that Jordanian army officers and police hold key positions in the defence and internal security forces of Qatar. There is some discussion of the use of oil prices as a weapon against countries supporting Israel.

251 **The Union of Arab Amirates.**
John Duke Anthony. *Middle East Journal*, vol. 26, no. 3 (1972), p. 271-87.

An investigation into the creation of the U.A.A. and the nature of the individual emirates within the federation. Qatar's decision in September 1971 not to join the federation, but to opt for independent statehood, is mentioned.

252 **Recent developments in the Persian Gulf.**
H. G. Balfour-Paul. *Royal Central Asian Journal*, vol. 56, pt. 1 (1969), p. 12-19.

An analysis of the political responses of Bahrain, Qatar and the seven Trucial States to the changes taking place in the Middle East in the 1960s. Three groups of changes are considered: acts of foreign governments, the incorporation of the area into the mainstream of Arab life, and the continuous discovery of oil. Four needs are identified as being crucial in the mid-1960s: the creation of a greater sense of unity, the development of links with their neighbours, economic expansion to improve living standards, and the strengthening of their defences.

253 **The Persian Gulf.**
R. M. Burrell. Washington, DC: Center for Strategic and International Studies, Georgetown University (Washington Papers, no. 1); New York: Library Press, 1972. 81p. map.

An analysis of the impact of political change in the Gulf over the last twenty-five years. Qatar is mainly discussed in chapter 3, in connection with the circumstances of its achievement of independence from Britain in 1971.

254 **Politics and participation where Britannia once ruled.**
R. M. Burrell. *New Middle East*, no. 51 (Dec. 1972), p. 32-36.

An evaluation of the first year of independence in the Gulf following the British withdrawal of 1971. The February 1972 family *coup* in Qatar is briefly mentioned.

255 **Problems and prospects in the Gulf.**
R. M. Burrell. *Round Table*, 1972, p. 209-19.
An evaluation of the politics of the Gulf in the wake of Britain's withdrawal in December 1971. Attention is paid to the growth of Iranian power, and the proposed Federation of Arab Emirates of which Qatar was initially to have been part.

256 **British withdrawal from the Persian Gulf.**
Alvin J. Cottrell. *Military Review*, vol. 50, no. 6 (1970), p. 14-21.
This paper comments on the role of British troops in the Gulf as an aid to the maintenance of internal order within the individual states in the era before Britain's announced withdrawal. The proposed federation of the nine Gulf emirates including Qatar is also discussed.

257 **Conflict in the Persian Gulf.**
Alvin J. Cottrell. *Military Review*, vol. 51, no. 2 (Feb. 1971), p. 33-41.
The internal rivalries between the southern Gulf emirates and the possibility of political revolution within them are discussed in this paper. Two factions are identified within the Federation of Arab Emirates: Abu Dhabi supported by Bahrain, and Dubai and Qatar whose ruling houses are linked by marriage. The uncertainty over whether Britain was in fact going to withdraw, which existed as late as 1971, is also evident. The author suggests that Iran and Saudi Arabia would play crucial roles in the future of the area.

258 **Defending the Gulf: a survey.**
The Economist, 6 June 1981, special report. 38p.
An investigation into the geopolitics of the Gulf, in the light of the recent establishment of the US Rapid Deployment Force and the Gulf Co-operation Council.

259 **Persian Gulf - contrasts and similarities.**
Mohammed Reza Djalili, Dietrich Kapelier. *Aussenpolitik* (English edition), vol. 29 (1978), p. 228-34.
Provides details on the so-called facts, including sections on the territories, populations, political systems, military capability, foreign policy and economic situations of the countries of the Gulf, and on what these imply in terms of the Gulf as an oil regulator, unequal chances for the future, unequal power distribution, external interests and potential sources of upheaval. There are frequent mentions of Qatar.

260 **Persian Gulf countries at the cross-roads.**
G. Dymov. *International Affairs* (USSR), no. 3 (March 1973), p. 53-59.
An analysis of the future of Bahrain, Qatar and the United Arab Emirates after 'the collapse of centuries-old British colonial domination'. US interests in the Gulf, particularly concerning oil, are also discussed. The paper argues that 'Western plans are in line with the interests of reactionary circles, who seek to secure foreign support in their fight against the forces of national liberation and social emancipation'.

Politics

261 **Arabia: when Britain goes.**
Fabian Research Bureau. London: Fabian Society, 1967.
28p. map. (Fabian Research Series, no. 259).
Qatar is discussed in this pamphlet in connection with possible groupings of the
emirates of the lower Gulf after British withdrawal, and also in the section on oil.

262 **Iraq: emergent Gulf power.**
Edmund Ghareeb. In: *The security of the Persian Gulf.*
Edited by Hossein Amirsadeghi. London: Croom Helm,
1981, p. 197-230.
This paper on the growth of Iraqi influence in the Gulf notes that Iraq supported
the creation of a federation between the seven Gulf emirates, Qatar and Bahrain,
which it viewed as a fence protecting the Gulf from imperialism.

263 **Gulf states: a special supplement.**
International Herald Tribune, July 1981. 4p.
A report on the Gulf Co-operation Council established in May 1981 by Bahrain,
Kuwait, Oman, Qatar, Saudi Arabia and the United Arab Emirates. It argues
that the cautious and conservative development policy of Qatar is paying
dividends in both the political and economic spheres.

264 **Arabia without sultans.**
Fred Halliday. Harmondsworth, England: Penguin, 1974.
Reprinted, with postscript, 1979. 528p. 16 maps.
A book on revolutionary activity in Arabia. Qatar is mentioned in chapters 12
and 13 on oil and the smaller states of the Gulf.

265 **Federation and the future of the Gulf.**
Nicholas Herbert. *Mid East*, vol. 8, no. 6 (1968), p. 10-14.
An analysis of the potential for federation in the Gulf. Qatar's signature of the
Exclusive Treaties with Britain in 1916 and its later participation in the Trucial
States Development Scheme are mentioned. A number of alternatives to future
federation of the Arabian states adjoining the Gulf are evaluated.

266 **The Annual Register: a Record of World Events.**
Currently edited by H. V. Hodson. London: Longman,
1758- . annual.
A brief summary of events throughout the world. All recent issues have included
a section on the year's events in Qatar.

267 **The Persian Gulf after the British Raj.**
David Holden. *Foreign Affairs*, vol. 49, no. 4 (1971), p.
721-35.
This evaluation of the politics of the Gulf at the time of the British withdrawal in
1971 notes the incorporation of Qatar into the perpetual maritime truce with
Britain. It suggests, as it turns out incorrectly, that the Union of Arab Emirates
would be a short-lived institution.

268 **The Arabian peninsula: society and politics.**
Edited by Derek Hopwood. London: George Allen &
Unwin, 1972. 320p.

A selection of papers on the society and politics of the Arabian peninsula that
were presented to a joint seminar and conference organized by the Centre of
Middle Eastern Studies at the School of Oriental and African Studies, University
of London, and the Middle East Centre of St. Antony's College, Oxford, in
1968-69. The papers by Abu-Hakima (chapter 2), Stoakes (chapter 9), Penrose
(chapter 13), and Sayigh (chapter 14) include mentions of Qatar mainly in the
context of its role as an oil-producing state.

269 **Ferment on the Persian Gulf.**
Arnold Hottinger. *Swiss Review of World Affairs*, vol. 20,
no. 2 (Feb. 1971), p. 12-16.

An evaluation of the antagonism between Iran and the Arabian Gulf states early
in 1971. Some discussion of Britain's wishes to form a union of the nine coastal
states, including Qatar, is included.

270 **The Persian Gulf after Iran's revolution.**
J. C. Hurewitz. New York: Foreign Policy Association,
1979. 64p. 2 maps. bibliog. (Headline Series, no. 244).

This pamphlet traces the political emergence of the states of the Gulf and in
particular the potential for change following Iran's 1979 revolution. Details of
Qatar's oil revenues are provided, and it is noted that a large percentage of its
population consists of foreign labour. The departure of British power in 1971 is
seen as having led to a situation of balanced instability in the Gulf, and the fall
of the Shah of Iran as having led to a power vacuum.

271 **The Persian Gulf: British withdrawal and Western security.**
J. C. Hurewitz. *Annals of the American Academy of
Political and Social Science*, no. 401 (May 1972), p.
106-15.

An essentially cautious evaluation of the likely outcome of British withdrawal
from the Gulf, which notes the considerable importance of this region as an oil
supplier to the Western world. It is written largely as a review of previous British
activity in the region. It records that Britain took over the external sovereignty of
Qatar in 1916 and that the ruler agreed to issue no concessions without British
consent. It also notes Qatar's independence, declared on 3 September 1971, and
its admission to the United Nations on 21 September of the same year.

272 **The Persian Gulf: prospects for stability.**
J. C. Hurewitz. New York: Foreign Policy Association,
1974. 64p. 2 maps. (Headline Series, no. 220).

This study analyses the political side-effects of what was seen in the early 1970s
as an emerging oil crisis. Qatar is seen as one of the minor states in the region.
Details are provided of the British loss of influence in the area and the subsequent state of balanced instability that prevailed. One chapter investigates Soviet
interests in the Gulf, and another specific US policies relating to the area. There
are frequent scattered mentions of Qatar.

Politics

273 **The future in Arabia.**
John B. Kelly. *International Affairs* (UK), vol. 42, no. 4
(Oct. 1966), p. 619-40.
The author of this article was of the opinion that there was no credible alternative to shaikhly rule visible in Qatar in the 1960s. Although revolutionary change may have had some relevance to Kuwait and Bahrain it was seen as having none to the Trucial Coast and Qatar.

274 **The United Arab Emirates: unity in fragmentation.**
Ali Mohammed Khalifa. Boulder, Colorado: Westview
Press; London: Croom Helm, 1979. 235p. 6 maps. bibliog.
This study attempts to trace the background, consummation, and development of the UAE as a federal entity in a primarily tribal culture. Qatar is mentioned in connection with its contributions to the Development Fund, established in the mid-1960s by the Trucial States Council, and with the early negotiations when it was planned that Qatar would be part of a wider Gulf federation. The rivalry between Bahrain and Qatar is seen as one of the main factors leading to their subsequent individual independence.

275 **Oil politics in the Persian Gulf region.**
M. A. Saleem Khan. *India Quarterly*, vol. 30 (1974), p.
25-41.
Studies the oil politics of the Gulf in terms of the energy crisis, and the use of oil as a political weapon. Most attention is paid to the collective policies of OPEC, but there are some specific mentions of Qatar.

276 **Revolution in the Gulf.**
Helen Lackner. *Race*, vol. 15 (1974), p. 515-27.
Although this paper is mainly concerned with revolution in Oman, Qatar is briefly mentioned in a section on the British withdrawal from the Gulf.

277 **Il petrolio nella geografia politica della penisola d'Arabia.**
(The political geography of oil in the Arabian peninsula.)
V. Langella. *Annali, Instituto Orientale di Napoli*, vol. 14,
pt. 1 (1964), p. 203-32.
An analysis of the political geography of oil in Arabia. It includes frequent mentions of Qatar.

278 **Gulf union.**
David Ledger. *Middle East International*, no. 9 (Dec.
1971), p. 6-7, 44.
A prediction that following the British withdrawal from the Gulf the political future of the region would be stormy. It notes Qatar's independence, and argues that it has a settled political situation in contrast to many other states in the region.

279 Britain's withdrawal.
William Luce. *Survival*, vol. 11, no. 6 (June 1969), p. 186-92.

The author argues that prior to 1948 British interests in the Gulf arose largely from her interests in India, but that after this date the presence of oil in the region became of dominant significance. He suggests that the chances of local conflicts and Russian intervention would have been increased by the British withdrawal in 1971.

280 The Middle East.
London: IC Publications, May-June 1974- . monthly.

Covers a wide range of political and economic issues, and also includes useful book reviews.

281 Middle East Newsletters: Gulf States, Iraq, Iran, Kuwait, Bahrain, Qatar, United Arab Emirates, Oman.
London: IC Publications, 1 Dec. 1980- . fortnightly.

Formerly *Middle East Newsletter*. Includes sections on politics and defence; economy and trade; oil, energy and minerals; and banking, finance and aid.

282 The changing balance of power in the Persian Gulf.
Elizabeth Monroe. New York: American Universities Field Staff, 1972. 79p. 2 maps. bibliog.

The report of an international seminar at the Center for Mediterranean Studies in Rome in the summer of 1972. It begins with a summary of the political and social background of the area, before discussing oil, internal problems, and the Soviet and Chinese 'problems'. It includes several scattered references to Qatar.

283 Conflict and cooperation in the Persian Gulf.
Edited by Mohammed Mughisuddin. New York, London: Praeger, 1977. 192p. (Praeger Special Studies in International Politics and Government).

This book analyses three levels of co-operation and conflict in the Gulf: the domestic, the sub-systemic, and the systemic levels. Qatar is discussed in the papers by Anderson, Van Atta, Hazelwood, Said, and McLaurin.

284 Qatar: a special supplement.
International Herald Tribune, June 1981, p. 7s-10s.

A special report commenting on Qatar's role as the main promoter and supporter of the concept of Gulf co-operation. It also includes details of Qatar's economy, sports facilities, medical services, and fishing industries.

Politics

285 **The Persian Gulf and the Strait of Hormuz.**
Rouhollah K. Ramazani. Alphen aan den Rijn,
Netherlands: Sijthoff & Noordhoff, 1979. 180p. 2 maps.
(International Straits of the World, vol. 3).

An analysis of the potential for conflict or co-operation in a waterway through which passes much of the world's oil. Qatar is noted as an oil exporter with a high percentage of expatriate labour. The dispute between Qatar and Bahrain over the Hawar Islands, which was on the agenda of the July 1975 Islamic Conference in Jiddah, is also mentioned (p. 110 and 127).

286 **L'Arabie à l'âge du petrole.** (Arabia in the oil age.)
Edouard Sablier. *Table Ronde*, vol. 126 (June 1958), p.
145-60.

An investigation into the politics of Arabia, written soon after the beginnings of major oil developments in the area. Particular attention is paid to the Buraimi dispute. The extravagant uses to which oil revenue was put by the emirs of Katar are noted.

287 **Bahrain, Qatar, and the United Arab Emirates: colonial past, present problems, and future prospects.**
Muhammad T. Sadik, William P. Snavely. Toronto,
London: Lexington Books, 1972. 255p. map. bibliog.

A detailed evaluation of the political development of the nine city states that became Bahrain, Qatar and the United Arab Emirates in 1971. It begins with an historical overview, from the Portuguese control of the Strait of Hormuz in the 16th century to the problems of federation faced by the Gulf states in the 1970s. Although the following chapters on the economic, social and political foundations relate to the area as a whole, they provide much information specifically related to Qatar. The ninety-seven tables similarly provide an extensive description of the socio-economic structure of the region. The final four chapters discuss the general processes of federation, and argue that the best prospects for the future lie in the federation of all of the nine states. With the benefit of hindsight it is clear that the differences between Qatar, Bahrain and the other emirates were too great to permit this.

288 **Conflict and cooperation in the Gulf.**
K. R. Singh. *International Studies* (India), vol. 15, no. 4
(1976), p. 487-508.

A study of the regional politics of the Gulf following the British withdrawal of 1971. The Buraimi Oasis and Khor al-Udaid dispute between Saudi Arabia, Qatar, Abu Dhabi and Oman, which was eventually resolved in 1974, is mentioned. There is also a discussion of the rival claims of Bahrain and Qatar to the Island of Huwar. Most of the paper, though, is involved with an analysis of the tensions between Iran and Iraq.

289 **Social and political change in the Third World: some peculiarities of oil-producing principalities of the Persian Gulf.**
Frank Stoakes. In: *The Arabian peninsula: society and politics.* Edited by Derek Hopwood. London: George Allen & Unwin, 1972, p. 189-215.
A study of the political organization resulting from the nature of the Gulf states as oil-producing principalities. In Qatar the replacement of a merchant oligarchy by one leading family under the recognition of the Ottomans and the British authorities in the late 19th century is noted. The 1963 strike representing the rebellion of aristocratic village families against the Al Thani monopoly in Qatar is also mentioned. Qatar is seen as being exceptional among the Gulf states in that Wahhabism has helped to build an ideological bond between rulers and the public.

290 **The Persian Gulf region.**
Roy E. Thoman. *Current History*, no. 353, vol. 60 (1971), p. 38-45.
An evaluation of regional power politics in the Gulf. The article notes the provisional constitution for Qatar promulgated in April 1971, providing for an advisory council as well as a cabinet. It argues that, although the al-Thani family continues to monopolize political power, serious unrest is unlikely due to the relatively high standard of living.

291 **The Arabs, the Heath government and the future of the Gulf.**
D. C. Watt. *New Middle East*, no. 30 (1971), p. 25-27.
A study of the attitudes of Arab states, particularly Egypt, to the political manoeuvres behind Britain's planned withdrawal from the Gulf, and the emergence of a federation of the smaller Gulf states.

292 **The changed balance of power in the Persian Gulf.**
D. Wright. *Asian Affairs*, vol. 60, pt. 3 (Oct. 1973), p. 255-62.
An investigation into the British involvement in the Gulf, and the effects of withdrawal in 1971. It includes several incidental mentions of Qatar.

293 **The Gulf in the 1980s.**
Valerie Yorke. London: Royal Institute of International Affairs, 1980. 80p. map. (Chatham House Papers, no. 6).
An analysis of policy options towards the Gulf for the West in the aftermath of the Iranian revolution of 1979, and in the light of the importance of this region as an oil producer. It assesses the various sources of political instability as they are seen by the Gulf states themselves. Qatar is specifically discussed on p. 30-32, where its limited oil reserves are seen as a major source of problems in the future. Its support of the Palestine Liberation Organization and the provision of education facilities for Palestinians are highlighted, and regional co-operation is seen as an important key to Qatar's internal security.

Qatar and its people.
See item no. 21.

Politics

The Persian Gulf: an introduction to its peoples, politics, and economics.
See item no. 24.

Political geography of Trucial Oman and Qatar.
See item no. 86.

The United Arab Emirates: a modern history.
See item no. 157.

Britain and the Gulf - don't go just yet please!: the wisdom of withdrawal reconsidered.
See item no. 167.

The Bahrein islands (750-1951): a contribution to the study of power politics in the Persian Gulf.
See item no. 174.

Arabia, the Gulf and the West.
See item no. 187.

India and the Persian Gulf region, 1858-1907: a study in British imperial policy.
See item no. 191.

Gulf states.
See item no. 192.

The Middle East: a political and economic survey.
See item no. 197.

Persian Gulf oil in Middle East and international conflicts.
See item no. 308.

The Persian Gulf and Indian Ocean in international politics.
See item no. 309.

Policies of the Arab littoral states in the Persian Gulf region.
See item no. 310.

U.S. supports admission of Qatar to the United Nations.
See item no. 311.

The superpowers in the Persian Gulf region.
See item no. 312.

Iran, the Arabs and the Persian Gulf.
See item no. 313.

OPEC and the industrial world - prospects for co-operation.
See item no. 318.

Eastern Arabian frontiers.
See item no. 320.

Sovereignty and jurisdiction in eastern Arabia.
See item no. 321.

Confrontation: the Middle East and world politics.
See item no. 322.

The struggle for the Middle East.
See item no. 323.

Soviet policy in the Persian Gulf.
See item no. 326.

The Persian Gulf and international relations.
See item no. 327.

Boundaries and petroleum developments in southern Arabia.
See item no. 329.

Oil and the evolution of boundaries in eastern Arabia.
See item no. 330.

Political boundaries and nomadic grazing.
See item no. 331.

Arab-American relations in the Persian Gulf.
See item no. 333.

Moscow and the Persian Gulf countries.
See item no. 335.

The U.S.S.R. and Arabia: the development of Soviet policies and attitudes towards the countries of the Arabian peninsula.
See item no. 336.

Géopolitique du pétrole et stratégie des grandes puissances dans le golfe Persique. (The geopolitics of oil and the strategy of the great powers in the Persian Gulf.)
See item no. 337.

A view from the Rimland: an appraisal of Soviet interests and involvement in the Gulf.
See item no. 338.

Security in the Persian Gulf.
See item no. 340.

Moscow and the Persian Gulf: an analysis of Soviet ambitions and potential.
See item no. 341.

Policies of Iran in the Persian Gulf region.
See item no. 342.

In the direction of the Persian Gulf. The Soviet Union and the Persian Gulf.
See item no. 343.

Energy policies of the world: Arab states of the Persian Gulf.
See item no. 350.

Middle East International.
See item no. 366.

Rim of prosperity. The Gulf: a survey.
See item no. 393.

Oil and state in Arabia.
See item no. 459.

The preliminary oil concessions in Trucial Oman, 1922-1939.
See item no. 465.

Middle Eastern oil and the Western world: prospects and problems.
See item no. 467.

The geopolitical significance of Persian Gulf oil.
See item no. 470.

Constitution and
Legal System

294 **The Arabian Gulf states: their legal and political status and
their international problems.**
Husain Muhammad Albaharna.   Beirut: Librairie du Liban,
1975. 2nd rev. ed. 428p. 9 maps. bibliog.
A revised and updated version of the author's *The legal status of the Arabian
Gulf states* (q.v.). Monographs at the end of the book contain the post-1968
developments. It provides detailed information concerning boundary disputes in
which Qatar has been involved, and on the emergence of the Arab Gulf states
following their independence in 1971.

295 **The legal status of the Arabian Gulf states: a study of their
treaty relations and their international problems.**
Husain Muhammad Albaharna.   Manchester, England:
Manchester University Press; Dobbs Ferry, New York:
Oceana Publications, 1968. 351p. 4 maps. bibliog.
A detailed analysis of the treaties and boundaries of the Arabian Gulf states.
Qatar is mentioned in connection with Britain in chapter 4, where the 1868 and
1916 agreements and the Anglo-Turkish disputes at the end of the 19th century
are discussed. The judicial and administrative systems in existence in the 1960s
are summarized on p. 12-16, and the boundary problems between Qatar and
Saudi Arabia and Abu Dhabi are also analysed later in the book. Chapter 17 on
offshore boundaries, a source of conflict due to oil prospecting and production,
discusses the disputes between Qatar and Bahrain, and also the Abu Dhabi-Qatar
dispute over Halul and other small islands.

296 Qatar.
Husain Muhammad Al-Baharna. In: *International
encyclopedia of comparative law.* Chief editor Viktor Knapp.
The Hague: Mouton; Tubingen, GFR: J. C. B. Mohr, vol. 1,
1972, p. Q1-Q4.
Provides information on the constitutional system and the sources and contents of
law in Qatar, written by the minister of state and legal adviser to the government
of Bahrain.

**297 Legal development in Arabia. A selection of articles and
addresses on the Arabian Gulf.**
W. M. Ballantyne. London: Graham & Trotman, 1980.
125p.
Numerous references to commercial and company law in Qatar are to be found
in this book. Much Qatari law has been taken from the Kuwait laws which are
based on an Egyptian/continental system. The Islamic *shari'a* (religious law)
forms the principal source of Qatar's legislation, and it is one of the Arab
countries of the Gulf which has a relatively large amount of written law. Qatar is
noted as being unique in the Gulf in terms of company law, in that it only
provides for joint stock companies.

298 The Middle Eastern states and the law of the sea.
Ali A. El-Hakim. Manchester, England: Manchester
University Press, 1979. 293p. 17 maps. bibliog.
This useful book, after a discussion of general practice and policies in connection
with the law of the sea, analyses specific regional issues. Within the second
section, details of the 1969 settlement of the offshore boundaries and islands
dispute between Abu Dhabi and Qatar, the 1970, 1972 and 1975 agreements
concerning the continental shelf between Iran, Qatar, the UAE and Oman, and
the continuing uncertainty over the offshore boundaries between Qatar and Saudi
Arabia, and Qatar and Bahrain, are summarized.

299 The Gulf states and Oman in transition.
Frauke Heard-Bey. *Asian Affairs*, vol. 59, no. 1 (1972), p.
14-22.
A study of the emergence of the Arabian Gulf states following the British withdrawal of 1971. Qatar declared itself an independent state in August of that year,
and is noted as the only state in the area with a properly published constitution.

**300 Administrative and legal development in Arabia: the Persian
Gulf principalities.**
Herbert J. Liebesny. *Middle East Journal*, vol. 10, no. 1
(1956), p. 33-42.
This paper analyses the development of British administration in the Gulf. Qatar's
status for the purpose of the British Nationality Act of 1948 was that of a
protected state, and it was administered by the Foreign Office. Three special
government departments, headed by British advisers, were established in Qatar:
the State Engineering Department, the State Medical Department, and the State
Police Department.

Constitution and Legal System

301 **British jurisdiction in the states of the Persian Gulf.**
Herbert J. Liebesny. *Middle East Journal*, vol. 3, no. 3
(1949), p. 330-32.
This paper provides details of the British Orders in Council relating to the Gulf
states following the Indian Independence Act of 1947. In Qatar British jurisdiction applied to all non-Muslim foreigners.

302 **Legislation on the sea-bed and territorial waters of the
Persian Gulf.**
Herbert J. Liebesny. *Middle East Journal*, vol. 4, no. 1
(1950), p. 94-98.
In May and June 1949 many Gulf states, including Qatar, issued proclamations
asserting their jurisdiction over the sea-bed adjacent to their coasts. This paper
provides some details of these arrangements.

303 **Iran, Saudi Arabia and the law of the sea: political
interaction and legal development in the Persian Gulf.**
Charles G. MacDonald. Westport, Connecticut; London:
Greenwood Press, 1980. 226p. 8 maps. bibliog.
This study focuses on the approaches of Iran and Saudi Arabia to the law of the
sea in the Persian Gulf as a study of the development of the law of the sea in
general. Particular attention is paid to the relationship between specific claims
and treaties and the underlying political interests that influenced these developments. The offshore agreements between Qatar and Iran, Saudi Arabia and Abu
Dhabi are mentioned in detail.

304 **Political participation and the constitutional experiments in
the Arab Gulf: Bahrain and Qatar.**
Emile A. Nakhleh. In: *Social and economic development
in the Arab Gulf*. Edited by Tim Niblock. London: Croom
Helm, 1980, p. 161-76.
An exposition on the thesis that evolutionary change in Bahrain and Qatar can
only come about peacefully through a process of internal political reform. It
includes a brief summary of the constitutional history of Qatar.

305 **Qatar.**
In: *Political handbook of the world 1977*. Edited by Arthur
S. Banks. New York: McGraw-Hill, 1977, p. 322-23.
Provides basic information on the country, government and politics, legislature,
news media, and diplomatic representation of Qatar.

306 **Qatar: agency legislation.**
London: Department of Trade, Commercial Relations and
Exports Department [n.d.]. 6p.
Provides details of legislation in Qatar relating to the appointment of Qatari
agents under law no. 12 of 1964 and its amendments.

307 **The legal framework for oil concessions in the Arab world.**
Simon G. Siksek. Beirut: Middle East Research and
Publishing Center, 1960. 140p. bibliog. (Middle East Oil
Monographs, no. 2).
This book examines the legal principles governing oil concession contracts in the
Middle East. Two case studies from Qatar are included: the arbitration award
between the Ruler of Qatar and Petroleum Development (Qatar) Ltd. in 1950,
and that between the Ruler of Qatar and International Marine Oil Company Ltd.
in 1953.

Politics in the Gulf.
See item no. 245.

The Persian Gulf region.
See item no. 290.

Selected Documents of the International Petroleum Industry.
See item no. 468.

**Selected documents of the international petroleum industry: Socialist
Peoples Libyan Arab Jamahiriya and Qatar pre-1966.**
See item no. 469.

Labor markets and citizenship in Bahrayn and Qatar.
See item no. 516.

Foreign Relations

308 **Persian Gulf oil in Middle East and international conflicts.**
Mordechai Abir. Jerusalem: Leonard Davis Institute for
International Relations, Hebrew University of Jerusalem,
1976. 35p. 2 maps. (Jerusalem Papers on Peace Problems,
no. 20).
This publication argues that the Gulf oil producers hold the key to the region's,
and possibly the world's, peace, and that there is more likely to be a clash of
interests between the Arabs and the West rather than between the Gulf oil
producers and the Soviet Union. Particular attention is paid to the influence of
the Arab-Israeli conflict on oil policy. The possibility of economic and political
co-operation in the lower Gulf, in which Qatar would play an important role, is
also discussed.

309 **The Persian Gulf and Indian Ocean in international politics.**
Edited by Abbas Amirie. Tehran: Institute for
International Political and Economic Studies, 1975. 417p.
A selection of thirteen papers and discussions on the Persian Gulf and the Indian
Ocean that were given at a conference in Tehran in March 1975. The papers by
Amuzegar, Burrell, Campbell, Stauffer and Taheri are of particular relevance to
Qatar.

310 **Policies of the Arab littoral states in the Persian Gulf region.**
R. M. Burrell. In: *The Persian Gulf and Indian Ocean in
international politics.* Edited by Abbas Amirie. Tehran:
Institute for International Political and Economic Studies,
1975, p. 227-48.
This paper concentrates on the internal political unrest of some of the Arab states
in the region. Qatar is briefly mentioned in connection with the 1974 territorial
settlement between Abu Dhabi and Saudi Arabia.

311 **U.S. supports admission of Qatar to the United Nations.**
George Bush. *Department of State Bulletin*, no. 1681, vol.
65 (Oct. 1971), p. 468-69.
The statement made by the US representative to the United Nations Security
Council on 15 September 1971 supporting Qatar's application for membership.

312 **The superpowers in the Persian Gulf region.**
John C. Campbell. In: *The Persian Gulf and Indian Ocean
in international politics.* Edited by Abbas Amirie. Tehran:
Institute for International Political and Economic Studies,
1975, p. 39-59.
An assessment of the involvement of the superpowers in the Gulf. Qatar is mentioned in connection with the British withdrawal.

313 **Iran, the Arabs and the Persian Gulf.**
Alvin J. Cottrell. *Orbis*, vol. 17, no. 3 (1973), p. 978-88.
An analysis of the influence of Iran, which is seen as the strongest local power
following the British withdrawal, in the Gulf. It suggests that Qatar needs a
respite from strife and conflict in order to permit the resolution of remaining
threats to its security.

314 **Military forces in the Persian Gulf.**
Alvin J. Cottrell, Frank Bray. Beverly Hills, California;
London: Sage Publications, for the Center for Strategic and
International Studies, Georgetown University, 1978. 72p.
map. bibliog. (Washington Papers, vol. 6, 60).
Qatar's military forces are discussed among those of the smaller Gulf states
covered on p. 50-52. Prior to independence in 1971 Qatar's defence was undertaken by the British task force stationed in nearby Bahrain and Sharjah. In 1977
the armed forces consisted of 4,000 troops, and in 1978 the ruler, Sheikh Khalifa
Ben Hamad al-Thani, became supreme commander of the country's armed forces.
The army consisted of two armoured car regiments, an infantry brigade and a
mobile regiment, while the air force was organized into a fighter unit and a
transport squadron.

315 **Combat fleets of the world 1976/77: their ships, aircraft and
armament.**
Edited by Jean Labayle Couhat, translated by James J.
McDonald. London: Arms and Armour Press Lionel
Leventhal, 1976. 575p.
Qatar's naval fleet is described on p. 319. In 1976 it consisted of six 103-foot
patrol boats, two 75-foot patrol boats, and three 45-foot patrol boats.

Foreign Relations

316 Mercenaries: "counter-insurgency" in the Gulf.
Fred Halliday. Nottingham, England: Bertrand Russell
Peace Foundation, for Spokesman, 1977. 80p.
Despite its title this book is almost entirely about the role of British 'mercenaries'
in Oman. There are, however, occasional references to Qatar, and it notes that in
1975-76 there were eight members of Her Majesty's armed forces serving in
Qatar.

317 Oil, debt and development: OPEC in the Third World.
Paul Hallwood, Stuart W. Sinclair. London: George Allen
& Unwin, 1981. 206p. bibliog.
This book argues that competition rather than co-operation tends to dominate the
relationship between OPEC members and the non-oil-exporting less developed
countries. There are frequent mentions of Qatar as an OPEC member. For example it is noted that in 1977 Qatar contributed over seven per cent of its gross
national product to aid, and that in 1974 it had the third highest per capita
income of OPEC members.

318 OPEC and the industrial world - prospects for co-operation.
Marwan Iskandar. In: *Issues in development: the Arab
Gulf states*. Edited by May Ziwar Daftari. London: MD
Research and Services, 1980, p. 202-09.
A study of the possible avenues for co-operation between the OPEC countries and
the industrial world. Qatar is used as an example of a country very dependent on
oil revenue, whose financial surpluses are largely in the form of bonds and bank
deposits.

319 Qatar pledges support for a Gulf federation.
Ralph Izzard. *Middle East International*, no. 3 (June
1971), p. 18-19.
The report of an interview between the author and Sheikh Khalifa bin Hamad
al-Thani, prime minister of Qatar and prime minister designate of the Federation
of Arab Emirates, who strongly advocated the formation of the federation.

320 Eastern Arabian frontiers.
J. B. Kelly. London: Faber & Faber, 1964. 319p. 2 maps.
A detailed study of the problems concerning the delimitation of the eastern boundaries of Saudi Arabia. The exploitation of oil is seen as the crucial factor
leading to the need for firm boundaries in this region. The 1949 Saudi territorial
claim threatened Qatar with the loss of a belt of land stretching from the Bay of
Salwah to the northern shore of Khaur al-Udaid, and threatened Abu Dhabi with
the loss of a much larger extent of land. The 1888-89 war between Qatar and
Abu Dhabi, after the Manasir had raided up to the walls of Dauhah and which
led to Jasim Al Thani sacking Liwa, is noted (p. 94-95). Qatar was firmly
defined under British control in the convention of 29 July 1913 in which the
Ottoman Empire renounced all claims on Qatar. The 1949 Saudi claims are seen
as being incompatible with the 1935 agreements in which Saudi Arabia and
Britain had agreed on the lands that were to lie within the Trucial Oman. The
Saudis claimed that since they received *zakat* (alms tax) from the bedouin at the
base of the Qatar peninsula this territory was rightfully theirs.

321 **Sovereignty and jurisdiction in eastern Arabia.**
John B. Kelly. *International Affairs* (UK), vol. 34, no. 1
(Jan. 1958), p. 16-24.

This paper mentions four territorial disputes involving Qatar: that between Saudi Arabia and Abu Dhabi over the coast and hinterland between Qatar and Abu Dhabi town, the dispute between Abu Dhabi and Qatar over Khaur al Udaid, that between Bahrain and Qatar over the ruined town of Zubara, and the dispute between Qatar and Saudi Arabia over their common frontier. It notes that the ruler of Saudi Arabia collected *zakat*, a form of tribute, from sections of certain tribes in Qatar and also pays them subsidies.

322 **Confrontation: the Middle East and world politics.**
Walter Laqueur. London: Wildwood House, 1974. 245p.

An evaluation of the 1973 Arab-Israeli war in which Qatar is mentioned as a member of OPEC in a chapter on the use of oil as a political weapon.

323 **The struggle for the Middle East.**
Walter Laqueur. London: Routledge & Kegan Paul, 1969.
360p. bibliog.

This review of Soviet policy in the Middle East during the 1960s briefly mentions Qatar's oil industry.

324 **International relations of Arabia: the dependent areas.**
Herbert J. Liebesny. *Middle East Journal*, vol. 1, no. 2
(April 1947), p. 148-68.

This paper mentions the 3 November 1916 agreement between the British and the shaikh of Qatar in which the former agreed to abide by the same agreements made with the other Trucial shaikhs. A further agreement in 1934 extended fuller British protection, and an oil concession was also granted to Petroleum Concessions Ltd. in the same year.

325 **United States policy towards the Persian Gulf.**
David E. Long. *Current History*, no. 402 (Feb. 1975), p.
69-73, 85.

This paper on US policy toward the Gulf following Britai:.'s withdrawal notes the historical relationships between Britain and Qatar, and the decision by Qatar to follow its own line of independence. It states that a US diplomatic mission was to be established in Qatar with political and export promotion responsibilities.

326 **Soviet policy in the Persian Gulf.**
R. D. McLaurin. In: *Conflict and cooperation in the
Persian Gulf.* Edited by Mohammed Mughisuddin. New
York, London: Praeger, 1977, p. 116-39.

This paper argues that Qatar has had less Soviet media attention than any other Gulf state, and that it is unlikely soon to become a major object of Soviet attention.

327 **The Persian Gulf and international relations.**
A. T. Mahan. *National Review*, vol. 40 (Sept. 1902), p. 27-45.

A general evaluation of the interests of Great Britain, Russia and Germany in the Gulf at the beginning of the 20th century.

328 **Arab-Persian rivalry in the Persian Gulf.**
John Marlowe. *Royal Central Asian Journal*, vol. 51 (1964), p. 23-31.

A paper mainly on the possibility of Arab unity and the conflicts between Persia and the Arabs, which includes a brief mention of Qatar as one of the states in the region of British hegemony in the period prior to the independence of India in 1947.

329 **Boundaries and petroleum developments in southern Arabia.**
Alexander Melamid. *Geographical Review*, vol. 47, no. 4 (1957), p. 589-91.

Although this brief report is primarily concerned with the Yemen/Saudi Arabia dispute, the unratified 1912-14 boundary between Saudi Arabia and the British-associated states including Qatar is mentioned.

330 **Oil and the evolution of boundaries in eastern Arabia.**
Alexander Melamid. *Geographical Review*, vol. 44, no. 2 (1954), p. 295-96.

A discussion of the problems of neutral areas in Trucial Oman, and the need for defining boundaries to enable oil exploration to take place.

331 **Political boundaries and nomadic grazing.**
Alexander Melamid. *Geographical Review*, vol. 55, no. 2 (1965), p. 287-90.

A brief account of the problems of boundary definition in areas of pastoral nomadism. Disputes between Qatar and Saudi Arabia are discussed, and the Manasir, living in Qatar, the Trucial States and Saudi Arabia, are used as an example of a tribe living in different locations at different times of the year, thus causing boundary delimitation difficulties.

332 **The Military Balance 1981-1982.**
London: International Institute for Strategic Studies, 1981. 133p.

Qatar's armed forces are summarized on p. 56 of this annual evaluation of the military forces of the world.

333 Arab-American relations in the Persian Gulf.
Emile A. Nakhleh. Washington, DC: American Enterprise Institute for Public Policy Research, 1975. 82p. 2 maps. (Foreign Areas Study no. 17).

An investigation into the relationship between politics and economics in the Gulf following the October War. It investigates three main dimensions: the political/ideological, the diplomatic/military, and the economic, and concludes with a framework for partnership between the United States and the Arabs. Qatar's path to individual independence is mentioned in the context of British withdrawal from the Gulf, and there are frequent mentions of the state in connection with oil and political organization.

334 Notes: Qatar.
Military Review, vol. 55, no. 9 (Sept. 1975), p. 97.

A note that Qatar has ordered twenty EE9 Cascavel armoured reconnaissance vehicles from the Brazilian company Engesa. These vehicles were modified in France and equipped with ninety-millimetre turret-mounted guns and night-firing devices.

335 Moscow and the Persian Gulf countries.
Stephen Page. *Mizan*, vol. 13, no. 2 (1971), p. 72-88.

An investigation into the cautious line taken by the USSR towards the Persian Gulf since the Arab-Israeli war of 1967. Soviet scepticism at the announcement in 1968 of British withdrawal from the Gulf, and the planned federation of emirates, including Qatar, is discussed at some length.

336 The U.S.S.R. and Arabia: the development of Soviet policies and attitudes towards the countries of the Arabian peninsula.
Stephen Page. London: Central Asian Research Centre, 1971. 152p. map. bibliog.

An historical analysis of Soviet interests in Arabia. According to the author, Soviet writers view Qatar's growing working class as a centre for the struggle for independence. Evidence for this was found in the May 1963 general strike, which was broken up by police, and in the formation of the National Liberation Front of Qatar and the Organization for the National Struggle of Qatar. Soviet policy, though, was initially against the formation of the Federation of Arab Emirates.

337 Géopolitique du pétrole et stratégie des grandes puissances dans le golfe Persique. (The geopolitics of oil and the strategy of the great powers in the Persian Gulf.)
Jean-Paul Pigasse. *Stratégie*, no. 19 (July-Sept. 1969), p. 47-91.

An analysis of the significance of the oil producing nations of the Gulf, situated at one of the most important strategic crossroads in the world, and their relationships with the USA and the USSR.

338 **A view from the Rimland: an appraisal of Soviet interests and involvement in the Gulf.**
Melvyn Pryer. Durham, England: Centre for Middle Eastern and Islamic Studies, University of Durham, 1981. 98p. 5 maps. bibliog. (Occasional Papers, no. 8).

A political geography of Soviet interests in the Gulf. Qatar does not feature prominently in Soviet policy, but it is noted as a state vulnerable to political unrest as exemplified by its so-called *coup*.

339 **The Persian Gulf: Iran's role.**
Rouhollah K. Ramazani. Charlottesville, Virginia: University Press of Virginia, 1972. 157p. 2 maps. bibliog.

A study of Iran's role, as that of the most prominent regional element, in the Gulf, set against the interests of the superpowers. Iran settled her territorial disputes with Qatar in 1969, and the relationship between Bahrain, Qatar and the Trucial States is seen as being critical to the effectiveness of Iran's interests in the area. Qatar's trade with Iran is mentioned on p. 86 and 89.

340 **Security in the Persian Gulf.**
Rouhollah K. Ramazani. *Foreign Affairs*, vol. 57, no. 4 (spring 1979), p. 821-35.

This paper investigates the question of who should maintain the future of the Persian Gulf. In particular it studies the possible role of the USA. It argues that a comprehensive economic and security partnership between a group of Gulf and OECD countries, thus including Qatar, would provide the best solution to the problem of peacemaking in the Persian Gulf.

341 **Moscow and the Persian Gulf: an analysis of Soviet ambitions and potential.**
O. M. Smolansky. *Orbis*, vol. 14, no. 1 (1970), p. 92-108.

This paper argues that on the surface the supposed direct advantages of Soviet control over the Gulf are minimal. It suggests that the short term policy of the USSR will be aimed at a gradual erosion of Western positions there.

342 **Policies of Iran in the Persian Gulf region.**
Amir Taheri. In: *The Persian Gulf and Indian Ocean in international politics.* Edited by Abbas Amirie. Tehran: Institute for International Political and Economic Studies, 1975, p. 259-78.

In this paper on Iran's political activity in the Gulf, Qatar is mentioned in connection with the British withdrawal. Iran is seen as having played a key role in preventing the British from implementing a federation of the nine Arab states of Bahrain, Qatar and the seven Trucial States.

343 **In the direction of the Persian Gulf. The Soviet Union and the Persian Gulf.**
A. Yodfat, M. Abir. London; Totowa, New Jersey: Frank Cass, 1977. 167p. 3 maps. bibliog.

An analysis of the Soviet Union's interest in the nations of the Persian Gulf set against the background of its relations with the Arab world, and the complexities of power politics. Qatar is mentioned in connection with the anticipated vacuum in the Gulf after the British departure (p. 71-73), and according to Soviet analyses it is thought to be a 'patriarchal-feudal' régime.

Conflict and cooperation in the Persian Gulf.
See item no. 283.

Economy

344 The businessman's guide to the Middle East.
Lillian Africano. New York; Hagerstown, Maryland; San Francisco; London: Harper & Row, 1977. 312p. map.

An introduction to understanding business in the Middle East, including sections on general information, doing business, and requirements before you go. Qatar is specifically discussed on p. 157-70, where the political structure, social climate, social welfare, economy, education, media, and development are surveyed, and details of currency, visa requirements and business hours in 1977 are given.

345 Persian Gulf oil and the world economy.
Jahangir Amuzegar. In: *The Persian Gulf and Indian Ocean in international politics*. Edited by Abbas Amirie. Tehran: Institute for International Political and Economic Studies, 1975, p. 321-45.

An analysis of the interdependence between oil-producing states in the Gulf, including Qatar, and the countries of the West.

346 The Arab Economist.
Beirut: Centre for Economic, Financial and Social Research and Documentation, 1969- . monthly.

A monthly publication of approximately fifty pages, which includes a business round-up, general economic reports, a financial report, a discussion of oil affairs, and a section on documentation on the Arab world.

347 Middle East economies in the 1970s: a comparative approach.
Hossein Askari, John Thomas Cummings. New York: Praeger, 1976. 581p. bibliog. (Praeger Special Studies in International Economics and Development).

This detailed book discusses oil, agriculture, industry, manpower, trade and the role of governments in economic development in the Middle East. Qatar is mentioned in detail in connection with oil, the industrial sector (p. 252-53), expatriate labour (p. 289-90), trade (p. 386), and planning (p. 443-45). It includes an extensive bibliography, and concludes that it is not in the long term interests of the Middle Eastern oil states to pursue a policy of confrontation with the industrialized countries of the world.

348 **Bahrain, Qatar, United Arab Emirates and the Sultanate of Oman: the businessman's guide.**
London: Standard Chartered Bank, 1979. 60p. map.
After a general introduction to the region each country is discussed in detail, with Qatar being analysed on p. 29-36. Information is provided on the state's geography, economy, government, immigration requirements, trade conditions, labour legislation, taxation and tariffs, transport and communications and general information, and it concludes with a section on useful addresses.

349 **Arab states of the Persian Gulf.**
Thomas C. Barger. In: *Energy policies of the world.*
Edited by Gerard J. Mangone. New York: Elsevier, vol. 1,
1976, p. 121-204.
Provides a geographical and historical background to the region, in addition to details of oil concessions and oil policies of the Gulf countries. Qatar's specific policies, as the smallest oil producer of the Arab members of OPEC, are discussed on p. 191-92.

350 **Energy policies of the world: Arab states of the Persian Gulf.**
Thomas C. Barger. Newark, Delaware: University of
Delaware, 1975. 93p. map.
This monograph provides a succinct overview of the land and peoples of the Gulf, an analysis of the production and pricing policies of oil, details of OPEC and its oil embargoes, and an analysis of the likely effects of future energy policy on the USA. Qatar is mentioned in numerous scattered references, and its specific oil policies are detailed on p. 79-80.

351 **Arab Business Yearbook 1980/81.**
Edited by Simon M. A. Barrow. London: Graham &
Trotman, 1980. 661p.
Part A covers pan-Arab data with sections on transport, telecommunications, banking, oil, population, construction and taxation in the Arab world. Part B provides country data, with Qatar being surveyed on p. 438-61. Here information is given on government institutions, the economy, finance, foreign investment, import regulations, development plans and oil.

352 **Development in the Middle East.**
Howard Bowen-Jones. In: *Change and development in the Middle East: essays in honour of W. B. Fisher.* Edited by
John I. Clarke, Howard Bowen-Jones. London, New York:
Methuen, 1981, p. 3-23.
This general essay on socio-political and economic change in the Middle East notes that Qatar's sovereignty has in the past been limited by foreign powers, and that it lies within the group of oil-exporting countries with relatively low short-run absorptive capacity.

353 **Major companies of the Arab world.**
Edited by Giselle C. Bricault. London: Graham &
Trotman, 1980. 5th ed. 731p.
A comprehensive coverage of Qatari companies is provided on p. 291-314.

354 **Issues in development: the Arab Gulf states.**
Edited by May Ziwar Daftari. London: MD Research and
Services, 1980. 224p. 3 maps.
A collection of economic analyses of the Arab Gulf states, which is divided into
three sections: bottlenecks, case studies, and viewpoints.

355 **Foreign Economic Trends and Their Implications for the
United States: Qatar.**
US Foreign Service, Department of State. Washington,
DC: US Government Printing Office, for the US
Department of Commerce, 1980. 11p.
An annual publication providing key economic indicators, an overview of eco-
nomic development, and information on Qatar's industry, infrastructure, services,
labour, transport and their implications for US businessmen.

356 **OPEC: its international economic significance.**
Girgis B. Ghobrial. In: *OPEC and the Middle East. The
impact of oil on societal development.* Edited by Russell A.
Stone. New York: Praeger, 1977, p. 65-101.
Qatar, the third smallest OPEC oil producer, is discussed on p. 83-85. Details of
industrial and educational developments are given.

357 **Business opportunities in ₊he Gulf states: Bahrain, Kuwait,
Oman, Qatar, U.A.E.**
Andrew Hayman. London: Metra Consulting Group, 1981.
246p. 7 maps.
After an introduction, summary, background discussion and analysis of the economy of the region, there are two chapters, on infrastructure, on industry,
agriculture and minerals, in which each country is studied in turn. The final
chapters analyse banking, trade, social services, investment, and the business environment in the Gulf. Appendixes include lists of useful addresses and contracts
placed by the Gulf states in 1980. It provides much useful information on the
economic changes that have recently taken place in Qatar.

358 **Gold rush economics: development planning in the
Persian/Arabian Gulf.**
Jared E. Hazleton. *Studies in Comparative International
Development,* vol. 13, no. 2 (1978), p. 3-22.
An evaluation of the options open to the countries of the Gulf for the use of their
greatly increased oil revenues following the price rises of 1973. Qatar is grouped
together with the other Arab oil-producing states of the Gulf as sharing a com-
mon background and thus a common development potential. The paper argues

that the gold-rush atmosphere may fail to provide a viable base for meeting long-term economic and social needs.

359 **Independent Qatar: MEED special report.**
Middle East Economic Digest, vol. 15, no. 50 (1971), p. 1,429-36.
This report produced almost a year after Qatar's independence provides details of its form of government, the evolution of the state, industrial growth, agriculture, social services and public amenities.

360 **The state of Qatar: an economic and commercial survey.**
Kerim K. Key. Washington, DC: K. Key Publications, 1976. 60p. 4 maps. bibliog.
A simple guide to the economic organization of the state of Qatar, aimed at the business community in the USA. It covers such topics as historical background, petroleum, finance, commerce, industry, agriculture, development, basic economic facilities, and social services. There are also sections on tourism and useful information for travellers, but these need updating.

361 **Oil revenues in the Gulf emirates. Patterns of allocation and impact on economic development.**
Ali Khalifa Al-Kuwari. Epping, England: Bowker, with the Centre for Middle Eastern and Islamic Studies of the University of Durham, 1978. 218p. map. bibliog.
This provides an analysis of the efficiency with which oil revenues have been utilized, with the aim of providing a better understanding for the future use of petroleum resources. Chapter 6 is specifically concerned with Qatar, and considers the allocation of the oil revenue in the period before 1965, the public expenditure and reserve, and the allocation of the state oil revenue since independence.

362 **Economic development of the Middle East oil exporting states.**
Keith McLachlan, Narsi Ghorban. London: Economist Intelligence Unit, 1978. 84p. map.
An evaluation of economic development in the oil states of the Middle East following the crisis of 1973. Trends in the petroleum sector, economic development between 1973 and 1978, and future economic prospects are analysed. Qatar is discussed mainly on p. 76-79. The high current levels of personal income enjoyed by native Qataris are seen as being likely to give rise to future problems. Almost all the projects designed to produce an income in the years ahead are seen as being based on oil and gas, either as raw materials or sources of power.

363 **Qatar, development of an oil economy.**
Ragaei el Mallakh. London: Croom Helm, 1979. 183p. map. bibliog.
This book aims to present the economic underpinnings of Qatar's present growth and future development, and views this within the framework of its oil industry. However, in addition, it provides interesting summaries of agricultural development, the organization of the communications network, education and health

Economy

facilities, and the banking system. It also studies Qatar's role in the international arena, paying particular attention to the organization of trade and the provision of aid to other developing nations. It concludes that Qatar is unique among the Gulf states in its moderate approach to economic development, and that despite its small population restricting market potential it has achieved much progress in this field.

364 **Oil exports and economic growth in the Middle East.**
M. M. Metwally, H. U. Tamaschke. *Kyklos*, vol. 33, no. 3 (1980), p. 499-522.

An examination of the role played by the export sector in the process of economic development of the major Middle Eastern oil producers. Although Qatar is not one of the sample countries studied in detail, because of the lack of information available to the authors, there are several passing references to the state.

365 **Middle East Economic Digest.**
London: Middle East Economic Digest, March 1957- . weekly.

A comprehensive weekly account of economic events in the Middle East, with both regional comments and sections on individual countries, including Qatar. It provides details of contracts, and there is also an annual review published in December.

366 **Middle East International.**
London: Middle East International, April 1971- . fortnightly.

A fortnightly publication of approximately fifteen pages covering current economic and political issues, and including book reviews and translations of several interesting documents.

367 **Claims to the oil resources in the Persian Gulf: will the world economy be controlled by the Gulf in the future?**
Farin Mirvahabi. *Texas International Law Journal*, vol. 11 (1976), p. 75-112.

This article presents an overview of the major legal issues relating to oil production in the Persian Gulf area. At the time it was written the major operating companies in Qatar were the Qatar Petroleum Company and the Shell Company of Qatar, both of which were sixty per cent owned by the government. The paper discusses the foundation of OPEC in 1960 and notes the later addition of Qatar to the organization. It also discusses aspects of the law of the sea in relation to the Gulf, and it concludes with a sector on economics, politics and the future, noting the political disturbances in Qatar.

368 **Modelling OPEC behaviour: economic and political alternatives.**
T. H. Moran. *International Organization*, vol. 35, no. 2 (1981), p. 241-72.

Qatar is mentioned in this paper on OPEC as a 'saver country'. Details of the 1976 Doha OPEC meeting are given.

86

369 **Persian Gulf studies.**
Emile A. Nakhleh. *Middle East Studies Association Bulletin*, vol. 11, no. 2 (1977), p. 31-43.
A report on the state of studies into the Gulf region, which includes a six-page bibliography. It notes that Qatar has a high percentage of expatriate workers in its labour force, and that the debate in the West over Gulf security has obviously been generated by Western needs for oil from the Gulf.

370 **Dilemmas of non-oil economic development in the Arab Gulf.**
Tim Niblock. London: Arab Research Centre, 1980. 18p.
(Arab Papers: Research Paper Series, 1).
A study of the economic development of Bahrain, Kuwait, Oman, Qatar, Saudi Arabia and the United Arab Emirates, concentrating on the dilemmas caused by the distribution of natural resources, reliance on migrant labour, the political requirement, the necessity for coordination and integration, and international investment strategies.

371 **The prospects for integration in the Arab Gulf.**
Tim Niblock. In: *Social and economic development in the Arab Gulf.* Edited by Tim Niblock. London: Croom Helm, 1980, p. 187-209.
A paper supporting the argument that economic integration is essential for the satisfactory development of the Gulf states. It discusses the co-operation between the future independent states before the British departure, the development of the federation of the United Arab Emirates, and the economic, social and political interchange and co-ordination between 1972-79.

372 **Social and economic development in the Arab Gulf.**
Edited by Tim Niblock. London: Croom Helm, 1980. 242p.
5 maps.
A collection of papers on socio-economic change in the Gulf presented at the inaugural conference of the Centre for Arab Gulf Studies at the University of Exeter, England. It focuses on the specific problems of social, economic and political development in the Arab Gulf region, and is centred around five dilemmas: the limits imposed by the resource base and the increasing dominance of the oil sector, the effects of economic policies on the demography of the region, the influence of a patriarchal form of government, the role of external international factors, and the relations between the Arab Gulf states themselves.

373 *OPEC Bulletin* **supplement: OPEC member country profile, Qatar.**
OPEC Bulletin, vol. 10, no. 16 (23 April 1979). 5p.
A brief introduction to the country covering its modern history, economic development and oil industry.

374 Qatar: MEED special report.
Michael Prest. *Middle East Economic Digest*, April 1977. 32p.

Provides details of Qatar's oil and gas, industry, banking and finance, agriculture, ports and transport, telecommunications, planning and housing, education and health, expatriate life, foreign relations, and future prospects. It concludes with a section on statistics, derived from the International Monetary Fund, relating to the years between 1971-77.

375 Qatar.
Arab-British Commerce, Oct. 1980, special issue. 24p.

An economic report on Qatar, paying particular attention to business opportunities in the country. It includes sections on oil, petrochemicals, banking, steel, trade, construction, the national museum, wildlife, the Qatar Investment Office in London and the Qatar Chamber of Commerce, in addition to basic information for businessmen and details of business procedures.

376 Qatar.
British Bank of the Middle East, Feb. 1979. 16p. 2 maps. (Business Profile Series).

A useful brief introduction to the economy of Qatar, including a statistical section and summaries of information for businessmen, visitors and residents.

377 Qatar.
London: Grindlays Bank Group, Economics Department, Sept. 1980. unpaginated.

A useful summary account of Qatar's economic structure, its recent developments, energy base, foreign trade, and economic outlook.

378 Qatar: a MEED special report.
Middle East Economic Digest, Aug. 1981. 52p.

Provides extensive details of Qatar's oil and gas resources, industrial incentives and projects, social services, agriculture, banking and foreign relations, in addition to some basic data on the state. In particular it gives detailed information on the planned development of Qatar's North Field gas reserves which are seen as providing the best revenue hope for the future.

379 Qatar: a society in transition.
Arab Economist, vol. 7, no. 76 (1 May 1975), suppl. 42p.

A supplement on Qatar, which includes discussions of economic co-operation in the Gulf, and Qatar's services boom, tourist industry, agriculture, budget, and oil and gas sector. It provides useful statistics on the state of the economy in the mid-1970s.

380 **Qatar: economic report.**
London: Lloyds Bank, Overseas Division, June 1980. 22p.
map.
A thorough account of Qatar's economy, which provides much useful information for British exporters. It includes sections on opportunities for exporters, currency details, import trade and regulations, investment and methods of payment, in addition to details of Qatar's industry, petroleum and gas production, agriculture, transport and communications, housing and social services, development aid, export trade and economic prospects.

381 **Qatar: *Financial Times* survey.**
Financial Times, 22 Feb. 1979, p. I-X.
Argues that Qatar's slow use of its oil revenue has avoided the worst excesses of the Gulf boom, and also comments on Qatar's general economy, politics, education, oil industry and banking system.

382 **Qatar: *Financial Times* survey.**
Financial Times, 22 Feb. 1980, p. I-VIII.
Provides details of Qatar's economy, industry, infrastructure, oil industry, gas reserves, trading, banking, education, and manpower, and also includes a section on Arabian myths. It suggests that, even when the oil reserves run dry, Qatar's development will be sustained by the huge discoveries of natural gas.

383 **Qatar: *Financial Times* survey.**
Financial Times, 16 Feb. 1981, p. I-VIII.
Comments on Qatar's heavy investment in infrastructure, industry and education, and suggests that the state's importance will be transformed by the development of the North West Dome gas field, which will make Qatar one of the world's largest gas exporters.

384 **Qatar: *Financial Times* survey.**
Financial Times, 16 Feb. 1982, p. 29-34.
A report on the ten years of growth and stability in Qatar, noting in particular that its gas reserves should ensure future prosperity. Detailed coverage is given to the economy, oil and gas, plans for broadening industrial development, education, infrastructure, defence, banking, business, the presence of Islam, and the development of new projects in the West Bay area of Doha. Some current statistics are provided.

385 **Qatar: l'activité économique est soutenue par les recettes pétrolières.** (Qatar: economic activity is maintained by oil revenues.)
Industries et Travaux d'Outre-mer, no. 326 (Jan. 1981), p. 49-50.
Provides details on transport, oil, the Umm Said industrial complex, and general commercial information for Qatar.

Economy

386 **Qatar: opting for stability and slow growth.**
Arab Economist, vol. 12, no. 128 (June 1980), p. 65-68.
This article, in an issue devoted to the economy and finance of Arab countries, discusses the planned slow growth of Qatar's economy set against the prospect that her oil reserves will be virtually depleted by the end of the 20th century.The Umm Said fertilizer, steel, petrochemical and natural gas liquids plants are mentioned in some detail.

387 **Qatar: the next stage.**
British Business, market report, 1980. 4p.
Published every twelve to eighteen months, this short report covers the main recent market trends in Qatar.

388 **Quarterly Economic Review of the Arabian Peninsula: Shaikhdoms and Republics.**
London: Economist Intelligence Unit, 1971-78. quarterly.
A quarterly review providing useful information on the economies of the countries of the Arabian peninsula. It has been replaced by the following item and two other publications on the UAE and Kuwait.

389 **Quarterly Economic Review of Bahrain, Qatar, Oman, the Yemens.**
London: Economist Intelligence Unit, 1978- . quarterly.
Provides a quarterly review and outlook of the economy of Qatar. An annual supplement is also published.

390 **Quarterly Economic Review of Oil in the Middle East.**
London: Economist Intelligence Unit, 1960-80. quarterly.
A review of current oil developments in the Middle East. It has been succeeded by the following item.

391 **Quarterly Energy Review: Energy in the Middle East.**
London: Economist Intelligence Unit, 1981- . quarterly.
A detailed publication mainly concerned with the economics o.̈ oil in the Middle East. An annual supplement is also published.

392 **Economics and political evolution in the Arabian Gulf states.**
Seif A. El-Wady Ramahi. New York: Carlton Press, 1973. 233p. 4 maps. bibliog.
A study of the changes that have taken place in the southern Gulf consequent on the exploitation of the oil reserves. Information is provided on Qatar's geography, history, government organization, oil developments, and industry.

393 **Rim of prosperity. The Gulf: a survey.**
The Economist, 13 Dec. 1980, special report. 84p.
An economic and political survey of the Gulf, paying particular attention to oil and the effects of the Iraq-Iran war of 1980-81. The section on education notes

that women students in Qatar outnumber the men. Qatar is also identified as being one of the few Gulf states which have 'the ability to say no, or not yet, to grand-sounding plans' (p. 63-64).

394 **Rising oil income in Qatar boosts economy.**
Africa/Middle East Business Digest, Aug. 1974, p. 4-7.
This paper provides details of Qatar's oil sector, economic development and social welfare programme, monetary and banking system, and external sector during the first half of the 1970s.

395 **The determinants of Arab economic development.**
Yusif A. Sayigh. London: Croom Helm, 1978. 181p.
A companion volume to the authors' *The economies of the Arab world* (Croom Helm, 1977). This volume is devoted to an analysis of the factors causing economic development in Arab states, and Qatar is cited as an example of a country where oil has been of crucial importance.

396 **Problems and prospects of development in the Arabian peninsula.**
Yusif A. Sayigh. *International Journal of Middle East Studies*, vol. 2, no. 1 (1971), p. 40-58.
Notes that the discovery of oil has drastically altered Qatar's economy, and that this has eroded the country's tribal structure and values. The problems for agriculture imposed by the state's physical environment are mentioned, as are the difficulties caused by its narrow industrial base. Qatar is seen as being behind Kuwait and Saudi Arabia in the achievement of social and economic overheads. The author argues that the political fragmentation of the region is absurd, and suggests that there should be a reallocation of resources to benefit the economic development of the whole region.

397 **Qatar as world economic power.**
K. Swamy. *United Asia*, vol. 21, no. 2 (1969), p. 102-06.
An analysis of the effects on Qatar of its membership of OPEC.

398 **The U.K. and Arabia: a commemorative issue to mark the visit of H.M. Queen Elizabeth II.**
Middle East Economic Digest, Feb. 1979, special report. 52p.
A survey of past and present economic relations between the United Kingdom and the Arabian peninsula. Most attention is paid to banking and the construction industry. It includes a useful summary of British trade with the Middle East between 1974-78, and a list of recent contracts with individual countries including Qatar.

Economy

399 Qatar.
United Nations Inter-disciplinary Reconnaissance
Mission. Beirut: United Nations Economic and Social
Office, 1972. 49p.

The second volume of the report of the UNESOB mission which visited Qatar in
December 1971 to study the economic and social structure and policies of the
country, to identify the major development problems, and to determine the prior-
ity areas for assistance. The mission concluded that the following fields of development required UN technical aid: the financial and services sector, large-scale
natural gas projects, export industries in co-operation with other Gulf countries,
import-substitute industries, small-scale industries for the domestic market, infrastructural facilities such as free zones and power and water facilities, and a sub-
regionally based industrial policy. The report includes twenty-nine statistical
tables relating to socio-economic conditions in Qatar *circa* 1971.

400 The social and economic evolution of Bahrein, Qatar, Muscat and Oman.
John J. Vianney. *Levante*, vol. 15, no. 1-2 (1968), p. 37-42.

Provides some general information on the development of Qatar under British
rule, from a country based on pearling and nomadism to one where oil provided
the major source of wealth. It notes the construction boom that began in the
1960s.

401 The Arabian Year Book 1978.
Edited by Rashid Wazaifi. Kuwait: Dar Al Seyassah Press,
1978. 964p.

The first edition of this publication listing details of businesses throughout the
Gulf states. A commercial and industrial guide to Qatar is given on p. 329-85,
and the book concludes with a who's who in the Gulf.

402 Qatar 1979: *Middle East Economic Digest* special report.
John Whelan, edited by Wilfred Ryder. *Middle East
Economic Digest*, Nov. 1979. 52p. map.

A detailed report on Qatar at the end of the 1970s, covering the following topics:
industry, employment, oil, gas, banking, contracting, water, agriculture, welfare,
expatriates and hotels. It also includes a list of contracts awarded in Qatar
between January 1978 and August 1979, and sections on economic indicators and
basic data.

403 The economies of the Middle East.
Rodney Wilson. London: Macmillan, 1979. 209p.

A study of the aspects of development in the Middle East which appear to the
author to be crucial in determining the region's economic activity. Qatar is discussed at length in chapter 5 on the Gulf, and its oil conservation policies since
1974 are noted. There is some speculation as to the potential for economic integration in the Gulf, and the problems of massive immigration are noted.

404 **Middle East focus: the Persian Gulf.**
Edited by T. Cuyler Young. Princeton, New Jersey:
Princeton University Conference, 1969. 220p.
This volume of the proceedings of the twentieth annual Near East Conference
includes thirteen papers and numerous discussions on the Gulf. It is divided into
four main sections: the historical background, oil-related problems, general economic problems, and socio-political problems.

Qatar and its people.
See item no. 21.

**Kuwait, Bahrain, Qatar, Oman, Arabemiraten. En guide för affarsmän
och turister.** (Kuwait, Bahrain, Qatar, Oman and the United Arab
Emirates. A guide for businessmen and tourists.)
See item no. 23.

Natural resources and development in the Gulf states.
See item no. 85.

**Qatar: special presentation by the government of Qatar on the occasion
of the inauguration of the Qatar National Museum.**
See item no. 147.

Bahraini strategy for prosperity.
See item no. 168.

The Middle East: a political and economic survey.
See item no. 197.

The United Arab Emirates: an economic and social survey.
See item no. 232.

Oil, power and politics: conflict in Arabia, the Red Sea and the Gulf.
See item no. 243.

The Middle East.
See item no. 280.

**Middle East Newsletters: Gulf States, Iraq, Iran, Kuwait, Bahrain, Qatar,
United Arab Emirates, Oman.**
See item no. 281.

**Bahrain, Qatar, and the United Arab Emirates: colonial past, present
problems, and future prospects.**
See item no. 287.

Focus on Qatar.
See item no. 407.

Talib's OPEC trade directory.
See item no. 417.

An economic survey of Qatar 1969-1973.
See item no. 518.

Economic survey of Qatar. Years 1976 and 1977.
See item no. 520.

Education in Kuwait, Bahrain and Qatar: an economic assessment.
See item no. 525.

Finance and Banking

405 Banking and investment 1980: *Khaleej Times* special report.
Khaleej Times (Dubai), 9 Dec. 1980. 30p.
A report on banking in the lower Gulf paying particular attention to the UAE and Bahrain but also of relevance to Qatar.

406 Banking in the Gulf.
Kevin G. Fenelon. *Banker*, vol. 120 (Nov. 1970), p. 1,198-210.
Banking in Qatar is discussed mainly on p. 1,209 of this article. In 1970 there were five banks operating in Qatar: the British Bank of the Middle East, the Eastern Bank, National & Grindlays, the Arab Bank, and the National Bank of Qatar. The paper notes that the total assets of these banks at the end of 1969 amounted to QDR 474 millions (£41 million).

407 Focus on Qatar.
London: Arab-British Chamber of Commerce, 1980. 36p.
Details of the proceedings of a conference held in London on 5 November 1980, which includes an economic and social overview of Qatar, information on trading relations with the UK, finance, development and industry, commercial banking, and some statistics.

408 Towards a Gulf Monetary Area.
Jawad Hashim. In: *Issues in development: the Arab Gulf states.* Edited by May Ziwar Daftari. London: MD Research and Services, 1980, p. 187-201.
The author argues that because of similarities in their economies it would be beneficial for Bahrain, Iraq, Kuwait, Oman, Qatar, Saudi Arabia and the UAE to form a Gulf Monetary Area. Qatar's high inflation rate, which it shares with Saudi Arabia and the UAE, is mentioned briefly.

Finance and Banking

409 **The development of banking in Bahrain.**
Alan E. Moore. In: *Issues in development: the Arab Gulf
states.* Edited by May Ziwar Daftari. London: MD
Research and Services, 1980, p. 138-53.
Although this paper concerns banking in Bahrain it also briefly mentions the note
exchange scheme between Bahrain, Qatar and the UAE.

410 **Qatar (3,67 riyals par dollar). Analyse et perspectives.** (Qatar
(3.67 riyals per dollar). Analysis and perspectives.)
Bulletin Commercial Banque Bruxelles Lambert, no. 7 (8
April 1980), p. 1-2.
An analysis of the economic and banking position of Qatar during the late 1970s.

411 **Qatar: le premier budget de l'indépendence.** (Qatar: the first
budget after independence.)
Economie des Pays Arabes, vol. 15 (1972), p. 12-15.
An evaluation of Qatar's first budget since independence, which argues that the
accession of Shaikh Khalifa ben Hamad al-Thani after the palace revolt of 22
February 1972 was a turning point in the country's economic history.

412 **Assessing policy options of oil-importing and oil-exporting
countries.**
Richard Van Atta, Leo Hazelwood. In: *Conflict and
cooperation in the Persian Gulf.* Edited by Mohammed
Mughisuddin. New York, London: Praeger, 1977, p. 79-102.
This paper identifies Qatar as an OPEC country which is expected to maintain
large annual revenue surpluses throughout the period 1975-85. It is thus theoreti-
cally one of the more powerful OPEC nations.

OPEC and the industrial world - prospects for co-operation.
See item no. 318.
Qatar.
See item no. 375.
Doing business in Saudi Arabia and the Arab Gulf states.
See item no. 420.
Trade and investment in the Middle East.
See item no. 422.
The rising costs of industrial construction.
See item no. 435.
The evolution of the oil concessions in the Middle East and North Africa.
See item no. 440.
Petroleum and the economy of the United Arab Emirates.
See item no. 457.

95

Trade

413 **Indo-Arab relations: an account of India's relations with the Arab world from ancient up to modern times.**
Maqbul S. Ahmad. New Delhi: Indian Council for Cultural Relations; Bombay: Popular Prakashan, 1969. 187p. bibliog.

A general account, written from an Indian viewpoint, of the cultural and economic relations between the Arabs and India, concentrating primarily on Egypt and Iraq. The Gulf is mentioned mainly in chapter 3 on trade and commerce.

414 **Bahrain and Qatar.**
London: British Overseas Trade Board, 1977. 96p. 3 maps. bibliog. (Hints to Businessmen).

Details on Qatar for visiting businessmen are provided in part 2, p. 44-76, of this useful account. In addition to general information on the climate, the economy and the society it provides detailed advice on travel and health requirements and the methods of doing business in the country. Details of hotels, telecommunications and import regulations are also provided.

415 **The past and present connection of England with the Persian Gulf.**
Thomas Jewel Bennett. *Journal of the Royal Society of Arts*, vol. 50 (13 June 1902), p. 634-52.

An analysis of the development of Portuguese and British interests in the Gulf, related to the expansion of trade with India.

416 **The Persian Gulf route and commerce.**
F. C. Danvers. *Imperial Asiatic Quarterly Review*, April 1888, p. 384-414.

This paper on the historical significance of the Persian Gulf trade route and the establishment of the East India Company's interests in the region notes the early 19th century capture of Zabara and Bahrein by the Imaum of Muscat.

417 **Talib's OPEC trade directory.**
Edited by Shamas Esmail. London; Basingstoke, England:
Macmillan, 1980. 679p.
The introduction provides general information on OPEC. This is followed by a
trade directory for all the countries within the organization, with Qatar's companies being listed on p. 549-81. A small section gives some details of Qatar's
history, economy and government.

418 **Hints to exporters: Bahrain and Qatar.**
London: British Overseas Trade Board, 1980-81. 76p. 2
maps. bibliog.
This useful guide provides general information on customs and behaviour in
Qatar, details of travel, hotels and telecommunications, a guide to economic factors, and thorough information on import and exchange control regulations and
methods of doing business in Qatar.

419 **The Gulf pattern 1977-1982: trade, ports, economies.**
Peat, Marwick, Mitchell & Co. London: Gray, Mackenzie
& Co., 1978. 129p.
This report considers economic trends in the Gulf and is in particular concerned
with maritime trade. Within each of the chapters on population, economic background, oil and gas, other industry, agriculture, trade forecasts, transport infrastructure and freight transport there is a special section on each country, including
Qatar. The authors consider that imports to Qatar will rise to about 1.5 million
dwt by 1982 and that the growth rate in imports of capital goods and construction materials is expected to exceed the ten per cent per annum of non-oil gross
domestic product. Details of the ports of Mina Doha and Mina Umm Said, which
include maps, are given on p. 113-14.

420 **Doing business in Saudi Arabia and the Arab Gulf states.**
N. A. Shilling. New York: Inter-Crescent Publishing and
Information Corporation, 1975 (with supplement 1977).
455p. 7 maps. bibliog.
A very useful study of the Arabian peninsula, paying particular attention to the
identification of markets; the economic frameworks in terms of laws and policies;
the incentives, advantages and pitfalls of business; and practical ways in which to
succeed in the area. Qatar is discussed on p. 247-87, with sections on the country
and its people, the government and political system, the economy, development,
foreign investment, business protocol, banking and finance, marketing, labour, and
general information. It suggests that of all the states in the area Qatar alone has
consciously sought to preserve the traditional Arab ambiance of its capital, Doha,
while also introducing modern amenities.

421 **Trade contacts in Arab countries.**
London: London Chamber of Commerce and Industry, 1976.
249p.
Part 1 provides a list of useful addresses, including embassies, high commissions,
and chambers of commerce in Arab countries. Part 2 is a directory of countries,
with details of Qatar's ministries, banks, industrial concerns and trading companies being found on p. 135-41.

Trade

422 Trade and investment in the Middle East.
Rodney Wilson. London: Macmillan, 1977. 152p.

This book analyses the internal and external implications of recent trends in trade and investment in the Middle East. Qatar is noted as a country which has not adopted import licensing, and which also has agreements on currency convertibility with Saudi Arabia, the UAE, Kuwait, Bahrain and Oman under Article 8, Sections 2, 3 and 4 of the International Monetary Fund agreement on convertibility. Qatar holds substantial amounts of its reserves in gold, and this is seen as a left-over from the days when it was an important centre for gold smuggling.

Special report: Qatar.
See item no. 47.

Spotlight Qatar.
See item no. 48.

From Oqair to the ruins of Salwa.
See item no. 123.

Bahrain, Qatar, United Arab Emirates and the Sultanate of Oman: the businessman's guide.
See item no. 348.

Business opportunities in the Gulf states: Bahrain, Kuwait, Oman, Qatar, U.A.E.
See item no. 357.

Qatar.
See item no. 376.

Qatar.
See item no. 377.

Qatar: economic report.
See item no. 380.

Qatar: the next stage.
See item no. 387.

Focus on Qatar.
See item no. 407.

Arab seafaring in the Indian Ocean in ancient and early medieval times.
See item no. 494.

The future of Gulf ports.
See item no. 495.

Industry

423 Engineering and development in the Gulf.
Bahrain Society of Engineers. London: Graham & Trotman, 1977. 228p.

Papers presented to the first seminar of the Bahrain Society of Engineers. The paper by Taheri on petrochemicals is relevant to Qatar.

424 Construction in the Arab world: a special report.
The Times (UK), 5 Sept. 1980, p. I-VIII.

Qatar is mentioned in scattered references in this report on the Middle Eastern construction industry.

425 Industrial development in Qatar.
A. S. Khudr. *Arab Economist*, vol. 6, no. 61 (Feb. 1974), p. 30-33.

This paper illustrates that Qatar has an overwhelming dependence on oil as the driving force behind its economy, and that the government is trying to diversify its industry. It notes that there are several serious impediments to industrial development, including a shortage of labour, its dependence on expatriates, its limited natural resources, the high wage levels, and its small domestic market.

426 Manufacturing industry in the lower Gulf, 1980: *Khaleej Times* special report.
Khaleej Times (Dubai), 17 Sept. 1980. 50p.

A report on the nature and extent of manufacturing in Bahrain, Qatar, the UAE and Oman. Qatar is specifically discussed on p. 43-44, where details of the Qatar Fertilizer Company, the Qatar Steel Company, the Qatar Petrochemical Company complex, and the National Cement Company are given.

Industry

427 Qatar.
Norsk Hydro, no. 2 (1978), p. 12-32, 38.

A special report covering the activities of Norsk Hydro in Qatar. It provides background information on the state of Qatar, and the lifestyles of Norwegians working there, but most of the report is concerned with QAFCO, the Qatar Fertilizer Company, for which Norsk Hydro is the co-ordinating engineer.

428 Qatar: achievements in industrial development.
Doha: State of Qatar, Industrial Development Technical Centre, 1981. 64p.

A thorough and complete account of recent economic development in Qatar. After introductory sections on history and geography, details are given on Qatar's agriculture, marine and coastal environment, the oil sector, natural gas resources and utilization, economic policy for industrial development, and incentives for industry. These general sections are followed by details of each major industrial project in the country.

429 Qatar: industrial and trade directory, exporters and importers.
Doha: Codco Establishment, 1977. 184p. map.

In addition to the directory covering commercial activities and a list of merchants, establishments, companies and their addresses, this includes an introduction on the history, industry, agriculture, social services, culture, and infrastructure of Qatar.

430 Qatar: industrialization before the oil runs out.
Arab Economist, vol. 10, no. 110 (Nov. 1978), p. 34-37.

An evaluation of the attempts made to diversify Qatar's industry to take up some of the slack when the oil runs out. Attention focuses on Umm Said.

431 Qatar projects list.
Doha: British Embassy, Commercial Department, 1981. 36+xiip.

An extremely useful publication for British businessmen, providing details of current projects in Qatar divided into sections on oil, government organizations and private business. It also gives lists of government contacts, contacts with other organizations, consultants, and contractors. Copies are available in England from Commercial Relations and Exports 5, Department of Trade, 1 Victoria Street, London SW1H OET.

432 Qatar: the ground laid for industrial expansion.
Middle East Economic Digest, vol. 18, no. 13 (1974), p. 352-54.

An analysis of Qatar's plans for industrial development. It notes the 1973 participation agreement which gave the government an initial twenty-five per cent share in the operations of the two major Western oil companies in the country, Shell (Qatar) and the Qatar Petroleum Company. It also discusses petroleum, the construction boom, the rise in imports, and the potential for co-operation with Bahrain and Saudi Arabia.

433 **Problems confronting the establishment of a heavy industrial base in the Arab Gulf.**
John Townsend. In: *Social and economic development in the Arab Gulf*. Edited by Tim Niblock. London: Croom Helm, 1980, p. 95-105.
A broad analysis of the use of existing resources for industrial development in the Gulf, including an appendix noting the present heavy industrial organizations and projects in Qatar.

434 **Industrial development in the Arab Gulf states.**
Louis Turner. In: *Issues in development: the Arab Gulf states*. Edited by May Ziwar Daftari. London: MD Research and Services, 1980, p. 210-20.
A paper assessing the potential future lines of industrial development possible in the Arab Gulf. It begins with a summary of the recent patterns of industrial development in each country, and Qatar is described as the state which is most enthusiastic about the industrialization route. Mention is made of Qatar's fertilizer, steel, cement, natural gas liquids and ethylene industries.

435 **The rising costs of industrial construction.**
Rodney J. Wilson. In: *Issues in development: the Arab Gulf states*. Edited by May Ziwar Daftari. London: MD Research and Services, 1980, p. 65-75.
A summary of the factors influencing increasing costs of construction in the Arab Gulf region. Brief mention is made of the Umm Said complex in Qatar. Rising land, rent and construction prices in the 1970s led to high inflation rates, and the weakness of the currencies against the mark and the yen have added to industrial input costs. The rapid increase of the Arab Gulf shipping fleets, which in Qatar occurred after 1975, is cited as one method of reducing external dependencies.

Doing business in Saudi Arabia and the Arab Gulf states.
See item no. 420.

Oil Industry

436 **Difficulties attending exploration in Qatar.**
J. Adler. *Oil Forum*, vol. 2 (May 1948), p. 178-79.
A brief summary of the seismographic survey undertaken by the Independent
Prospecting Company in Qatar, mentioning the Dukhan oilfield.

437 **The Middle East: oil, politics and development in the Middle
East.**
Edited by John Duke Anthony. Washington, DC:
American Enterprise Institute for Public Policy Research,
1975. 109p.
A collection of seven papers with commentaries, resulting from a conference
sponsored by the University of Toronto and the Canadian Institute of International Affairs in 1974. Qatar is mentioned occasionally, but, not being one of the
largest oil producers, its political voice is small.

438 **Aramco handbook: oil in the Middle East.**
Dhahran, Saudi Arabia: Arabian American Oil Company,
1968. rev. ed. 279p. 23 maps. bibliog.
Although this book is mainly concerned with Aramco's work in Saudi Arabia it
contains much interesting generalized historical material and numerous photographs. Oil developments in Qatar are discussed on p. 102.

439 **Wells of power, the oilfields of south-western Asia: a regional
and global study.**
Olaf Caroe. New York: Macmillan, 1951. 240p. 4 maps.
bibliog.
An analysis of the oilfields of the Persian Gulf. Qatar is described as a country of
sand-strewn monotony, and it is noted as one of the few countries in the Gulf
which by 1950 already had an appreciable production of oil.

440 **The evolution of the oil concessions in the Middle East and North Africa.**
Henry Cattan. Dobbs Ferry, New York: Oceana Publications, 1967. 173p. 2 maps.

This book is essentially concerned with the evolution of oil concessions throughout the Middle East, and with a comparative analysis of their juridical and financial conditions. It begins with an historical introduction, which notes the concession to the Anglo-Persian Oil Company in Qatar in 1935 covering the whole country. This is followed by an analysis of the financial and general conditions of oil concessions, and it concludes with a chapter on government participation in the oil industry. Appendix 1 lists the main oil concessions before the mid-1960s, noting those of Qatar on p. 159.

441 **OPEC and the international oil industry: a changing structure.**
Fadhil J. Al-Chalabi. Oxford, England: Oxford University Press, for OAPEC, 1980. 165p.

This book demonstrates the significance of the structural changes in the oil industry during the last thirty-five years in terms of their impact on the power of control and decisions concerning the ownership of oil resources, their marketing outlets, and price policy. Qatar became an OPEC member in 1961 and is often mentioned in the text.

442 **OPEC oil report, December 1977.**
Edited by Bryan Cooper. London: Petroleum Economist, 1977. 267p.

A thorough investigation into OPEC, covering the development of the organization, growth of oil revenues, oil prices, dependence of consuming countries on OPEC oil, transportation and movement of OPEC oil, natural gas and liquid natural gas, and export refineries and petrochemicals. It includes analyses of the oil industry in each member country, with Qatar being discussed on p. 218-25. Here information is provided on Qatar's land and offshore oil developments, the state's membership of OPEC, nationalization of the industry, and future developments.

443 **Expansion in Qatar.**
Petroleum Press Service, vol. 39, no. 9 (1972), p. 330-31.

A brief report on the emergence and growth of Qatar as an oil-producing state. It records production levels and details of the companies involved in exploration and production.

444 **Oil companies and governments. An account of the international oil industry in its political environment.**
J. E. Hartshorn. London: Faber & Faber, 1967. 2nd rev. ed. 410p. 5 maps. bibliog.

Qatar is briefly mentioned on p. 329 of this general text on the oil industry.

445 **The impact of the oil industry on the Persian Gulf sheikhdoms.**
Rupert Hay. *Middle East Journal*, vol. 9, no. 4 (autumn 1955), p. 361-72.
An analysis of the early social and political effects of the oil industry on Kuwait, Bahrain, Qatar, and the seven Trucial States. The lack of fresh water and cultivation in Qatar are noted. Petroleum Development (Qatar) Ltd., an associate of the Iraq Petroleum Company, began operations in 1938, but the first shipment of oil did not take place until 1949. Oil is seen as having provided an assured livelihood to all of Qatar's inhabitants.

446 **Petroleum developments in Middle East countries in 1979.**
D. O. Hemer, J. F. Mason, G. C. Hatch. *American Association of Petroleum Geologists Bulletin*, vol. 64, no. 11 (1980), p. 1,836-61.
Details of Qatar's oil production methods and development are given on p. 1,838-39.

447 **Oil and public opinion in the Middle East.**
David Hirst. London: Faber & Faber, 1966. 127p.
An attempt to provide a survey of Arab views on the oil industry in the mid-1960s. Qatar is mentioned as one of the member countries of OPEC.

448 **Prospects for gas prices and the development of the natural gas industry in Qatar.**
Ali M. Jaidah. In: *Issues in development: the Arab Gulf states*. Edited by May Ziwar Daftari. London: MD Research and Services, 1980, p. 154-59.
Gas was only discovered in significant amounts in Qatar in the 1970s, and its full reserves, although very large, have yet to be determined precisely. Various uses for these reserves, including desalination, aluminium and steel plants, and as a feedstock for petrochemicals, are suggested.

449 **The Japanese in Qatar.**
Petroleum Press Service, vol. 36, no. 6 (1969), p. 203-05.
Provides details of the concession obtained by Qatar Oil Company (Japan), which was initially acquired by Fuji Oil, Kansai Oil, Tokyo Electric Power, and Kansai Electric Power. These were later joined by a dozen other Japanese companies. The Japanese concession covered about 7,300 square kilometres off the east coast of Qatar.

450 **Oil in the Middle East: its discovery and development.**
Stephen Hensley Longrigg. London: Oxford University Press, 1968. 3rd ed. 519p. 9 maps.
A detailed account of oil discovery and development in the Middle East up to the mid-1960s. Qatar's early concessions are discussed on p. 105-06; the first well was spudded on the Dukhan structure in 1938. The physical environment of Qatar is frequently cited as being inhospitable. Oil developments in Qatar since the Second

World War are summarized on p. 314-17 and 417-21. The country is seen as being a particularly fortunate oil territory through the steady exploitation of its Dukhan field and the discovery of valuable offshore resources.

451 **The oil industry in the Middle East.**
Keith McLachlan. In: *Change and development in the Middle East: essays in honour of W. B. Fisher.* Edited by John I. Clarke, Howard Bowen-Jones. London, New York: Methuen, 1981, p. 95-112.
Qatar is mentioned frequently in this summary of the oil industry of the Middle East. Qatar's commercial lifting commenced in 1949, and the lack of other natural resources, associated with smallness of scale, have led to oil's continued dominance of the country's economy. The essay notes that in 1978 only seventy per cent of Qatar's installed production capacity was exploited.

452 **Oil production, revenues and economic development: prospects for Iran, Iraq, Saudi Arabia, Kuwait, United Arab Emirates, Oman, Qatar and Bahrain.**
Keith McLachlan, Narsi Ghorban. London: Economist Intelligence Unit, 1974. 59p. + postscript. map. (QER Special no. 18).
Qatar is discussed individually on p. 53-54 of this report on the state of the Gulf oil industry following the rapid increase in oil prices after October 1973. It notes that petroleum is the overwhelmingly dominant sector of Qatar's economy, and that outside the oil sector development has followed conventional lines, with heavy investment in public utilities, housing and hotels. It forecast that Qatar was unlikely to join the other Arab oil-rich states in joint financing organizations, but would rather move towards an expansion of the domestic oil-processing industries and welfare.

453 **New award in Qatar.**
Petroleum Press Service, vol. 37, no. 5 (1970), p. 173-74.
Provides details of the oil concession granted to Southeast Asia Oil and Gas Company of Houston, Texas, and also some information on Qatar Petroleum, Shell Qatar, and the Japanese consortium involved in oil exploration in Qatar.

454 **Oil industry in Qatar 1976.**
Qatar: State of Qatar, Ministry of Finance and Petroleum, 1976. 48p. 2 maps.
A thorough account of Qatar's oil industry covering its organization, the oil companies operating in the country, new petroleum agreements, the relation between Qatar, OPEC and OAPEC, and the contribution of the oil industry to the country's economic development. It concludes with a statistical section.

455 **OPEC Bulletin supplement: QGPC, Qatar General Petroleum Corporation.**
OPEC Bulletin, vol. 10, no. 49-50 (10-17 Dec. 1979). 24p.
Provides details of QGPC's exploration, production, reserves, refining, petrochemical operations, foreign marketing, finance and investment, and public relations.

Oil Industry

456 OPEC and the petroleum industry.
Mana Saeed al-Otaiba. London: Croom Helm, 1975. 192p. bibliog.
An analysis of the development of OPEC from its foundations in September 1960 to the early 1970s. Qatar is noted as the first country to join OPEC in January 1961 apart from the five founder members, and also as the smallest exporter of crude oil within OPEC. The book includes details of the internal structure of OPEC and of its policies with respect to oil prices, improving socio-economic conditions, and participation by governments within the wider oil industry.

457 Petroleum and the economy of the United Arab Emirates.
Mana Saeed al-Otaiba. London: Croom Helm, 1977. 281p. map. bibliog.
An investigation into the development of the oil economy of the UAE. The creation of the Bunduq Oil Co. in 1970 to develop the field traversing the marine boundary between Abu Dhabi and Qatar is mentioned, as is Qatar's membership of OAPEC. The agreement between Qatar and Dubai in March 1966 to issue joint Qatar-Dubai riyals, each worth 0.186621 grammes of fine gold, to replace the Gulf rupee, is also noted.

458 The golden bubble: Arabian Gulf documentary.
Roderic Owen. London: Collins, 1957. 255p. map.
An account of the author's journey in the countries of the Arabian peninsula adjoining the Gulf in the 1950s. Qatar is described in chapter 11. The author visited Qatar Petroleum Company's camps at Umm Said and Dukhan, and Shell's camp outside Doha.

459 Oil and state in Arabia.
Edith Penrose. In: *The Arabian peninsula: society and politics*. Edited by Derek Hopwood. London: George Allen & Unwin, 1972, p. 271-85.
An investigation of some of the effects of the discovery of oil in Arabia on the states within the peninsula. Oil was found in Qatar in 1939, but was not exploited until after the Second World War, when one third of the revenues were allocated to the shaikh, and the rest was reserved for public expenditure and investment abroad.

460 OPEC's importance in the world oil industry.
Edith Penrose. *International Affairs*, vol. 55, no. 1 (Jan. 1979), p. 18-32.
This paper notes that in 1974 Qatar imposed new royalty and tax rates, and limited company margins in the oil industry. It argues that as the OPEC countries increase their downstream production there is a need for European countries to enter comprehensive discussions with the members of OPEC.

461 **Arabian oil ventures.**
H. St. John B. Philby. Washington, DC: Middle East
Institute, 1964. 134p.
A collection of Philby's papers on oil in Arabia. Qatar is mentioned in connection
with the Hasa concession of 1923, as providing the northern boundary of the
concession in the agreement between Ibn Sa'ud and Holmes. The proposed 1933
Anglo-Persian Oil Company's survey of Qatar is mentioned in a letter from G.
M. Lees to Philby dated 7 December 1932.

462 **Qatar: entering the field of joint ventures.**
Arab Economist, vol. 11, no. 118 (July 1979), p. 22-23.
An evaluation of Qatar's contribution to the COPENOR petrochemical complex
opened at Dunkirk, France, in May 1979.

463 **Development of the oil industry in the Persian/Arabian Gulf
1901-1968.**
George Rentz. In: *Middle East focus: the Persian Gulf.*
Edited by T. Cuyler Young. Princeton, New Jersey:
Princeton University Near East Conference, 1969, p. 39-64.
An historical account of the growth of the oil industry in the Gulf. Qatar is
mentioned briefly as discovering oil prior to the Second World War, but as not
starting production until after the cessation of hostilities.

464 **Arabs, oil and history: the story of the Middle East.**
Kermit Roosevelt. New York: Harper & Row, 1949.
Reprinted, Port Washington, New York: Kennikat Press,
1969. 271p.
Qatar is mentioned briefly (p. 169) as possibly important for oil in the future.

465 **The preliminary oil concessions in Trucial Oman, 1922-1939.**
Rosemarie J. Said. *International Interactions*, vol. 3, pt. 2
(1977), p. 113-34.
An analysis of the political and economic factors influencing the granting of oil
concessions in the north-east of the Arabian peninsula. It includes discussions on
the D'Arcy Exploration Company, the Anglo-Persian Oil Company, Petroleum
Concessions Ltd., and California Arabian Standard Oil Company. Attention is
given to conflict between the American and British interests in the area, and
Qatar is mentioned briefly in connection with boundary disputes and as an example of a state where concession revenue relieved the economic depression of the
1930s.

466 **Arab oil and gas directory 1981.**
Edited by Nicolas Sarkis. Paris: Arab Petroleum Research
Center, 1981. 503p.
Qatar is discussed on p. 253-64 of this, the most extensive, source of information
on oil in the Middle East. Information is provided on the historical background,
reserves, production and export of oil, gas production and utilization, refining and

distribution, the petrochemical industry, terminals, pipelines and tankers, and the oil revenues of Qatar.

467 **Middle Eastern oil and the Western world: prospects and problems.**
Sam H. Schurr, Paul T. Homam, Joel Darmstadter, Helmut Frank, John J. Schanz, Jr., Thomas R. Stauffer, Henry Steele. New York: American Elsevier, 1971. 206p. 3 maps. (The Middle East: Economic and Political Problems and Prospects).
This book measures the interdependence between countries importing and exporting oil, and then the economic importance of oil to the exporting countries. Mention is made of Qatar's membership of OAPEC and her oil production and projected revenues.

468 **Selected Documents of the International Petroleum Industry.**
Vienna: Organization of the Petroleum Exporting Countries, 1966- . annual.
Contains the most important oil laws and regulations issued and agreements reached by OPEC member countries each year. Includes texts relating to Qatar, an OPEC member.

469 **Selected documents of the international petroleum industry: Socialist Peoples Libyan Arab Jamahiriya and Qatar pre-1966.**
Vienna: Organization of the Petroleum Exporting Countries, 1977. 176p.
Includes the most important oil laws and regulations issued by Qatar during the period prior to 1966.

470 **The geopolitical significance of Persian Gulf oil.**
Thomas R. Stauffer. In: *The Persian Gulf in international politics.* Edited by Abbas Amirie. Tehran: Institute for International Political and Economic Studies, 1975, p. 347-58.
An investigation into whether industrialization will benefit the oil-producing Gulf states, and to what extent the relationship between the Western world and these states, including Qatar, will change.

471 **Middle East oil: a study in political and economic controversy.**
George W. Stocking. Nashville, Tennessee: Vanderbilt University Press, 1970; London: Allen Lane, 1971. 485p. bibliog.
Qatar is mentioned in this general text in connection with its joining of OPEC and its increased production following the nationalization of Iran's oil industry.

472 **OPEC and the Middle East. The impact of oil on societal development.**
Edited by Russell A. Stone. New York: Praeger, 1977. 264p. (Praeger Special Studies in International Politics and Government).
A collection of papers deriving from a conference with the same title held at the State University of New York in 1976. Qatar is mentioned in a number of papers.

473 **Future of petrochemicals in the Gulf.**
M. Taheri. In: *Engineering and development in the Gulf.* Bahrain Society of Engineers. London: Graham & Trotman, 1977, p. 199-212.
This general paper provides some figures on oil production in Qatar.

474 **Oilfields of the world.**
E. N. Tiratsoo. Beaconsfield, England: Scientific Press, 1976. 2nd ed. 384p. 34 maps.
Qatar's oilfields are listed on p. 164-65 of this thorough text. Production commenced in 1950 from the only onshore field, namely the Dukhan field. Three offshore accumulations have been discovered and exploited at Idd-el-Shargi, Maydan Mahzan and Bul Hanine.

475 **Oil: the biggest business.**
Christopher Tugendhat, Adrian Hamilton. London: Eyre Methuen, 1975. rev. ed. 404p. 6 maps. bibliog.
The aim of this book is to explain how the oil industry works; it is largely historical in its approach. Particular mention of Qatar is made in terms of its membership of OPEC and its production levels.

476 **Oil, social change and economic development in the Arabian peninsula.**
John J. Vianney. *Levante*, vol. 15, no. 4 (1968), p. 45-48.
Comments on the development of the oil industry in Qatar and the consequent socio-economic change.

477 **Qatar fire. 'The big one everyone was afraid of'.**
John Whelan. *Middle East Economic Digest,* vol. 21, no. 15 (15 April 1977), p. 3.
An analysis of the fire and explosion at the Umm Said natural gas liquefaction plant, estimated as costing the insurance companies £40 million.

Oil Industry

478 **Plans underway to make Qatar a major source of petroleum.**
C. O. Willson. *Oil and Gas Journal*, 15 Dec. 1945, p.
80-81.

A summary of the geology and early development of oil survey in Qatar. The
exploitation of the Dukhan oilfield by Petroleum Development (Qatar) Ltd., who
obtained the concession covering the entire peninsula in 1935, is discussed.

The petroleum geology and resources of the Middle East.
See item no. 56.

Political geography of Trucial Oman and Qatar.
See item no. 86.

Qatar: a story of state building.
See item no. 159.

America and the Arabian peninsula: the first two hundred years.
See item no. 196.

Qatar: progressive puritans.
See item no. 239.

Oil policies of the Gulf countries.
See item no. 247.

Boundaries and petroleum developments in southern Arabia.
See item no. 329.

Oil and the evolution of boundaries in eastern Arabia.
See item no. 330.

OPEC Bulletin **supplement: OPEC member country profile, Qatar.**
See item no. 373.

Agriculture and Fisheries

479 **Agricultural development in Qatar.**
Salah A. Beheiry. *Journal of the Gulf and Arabian Peninsula Studies*, vol. 6, no. 21 (1980), p. 91-126. (In Arabic with English summary).
Despite the fact that 2,000 hectares of land have been brought under the plough, the future of agriculture in Qatar is gloomy because of increased soil and water salinity. Emphasis is now being given to improved cultivation methods and water conservation.

480 **Offshore politics and resources in the Middle East.**
Gerald H. Blake. In: *Change and development in the Middle East: essays in honour of W. B. Fisher.* Edited by John I. Clarke, Howard Bowen-Jones. London, New York: Methuen, 1981, p. 13-29.
Qatar's commercial fisheries are noted as an important offshore resource.

481 **The pearl fisheries of the Persian Gulf.**
R. Bowen. *Middle East Journal*, vol. 5 (spring 1951), p. 161-80.
A detailed account of pearling in the Gulf, which includes estimates of the number of boats involved in the trade in Qatar, the methods of pearling, and its influence on the economy of the region.

Agriculture and Fisheries

482 Agriculture and the use of water resources in the eastern province of Saudi Arabia.

Howard Bowen-Jones. In: *Issues in development: the Arab Gulf states.* Edited by May Ziwar Daftari. London: MD Research and Services, 1980, p. 118-37.

Within this paper specifically on Saudi agriculture, mention is made of the Neogene-Quaternary water-bearing rocks which extend into Qatar, and also of the fact that the vast majority of farms in Qatar are operated by tenants.

483 Agriculture in Bahrain, Kuwait, Qatar and U.A.E.

Howard Bowen-Jones. In: *Issues in development: the Arab Gulf states.* Edited by May Ziwar Daftari. London: MD Research and Services, 1980, p. 46-64.

A survey of the contemporary agricultural situation in Bahrain, Kuwait, Qatar and the UAE. In Qatar the cultivable land is only situated in a number of depressions, known locally as *rōdat*, of which only 3,800 hectares are classified as highly suitable for irrigation. The author notes that between 1958-67 the recorded number of demarcated farms rose from 40 to a peak of 461 from which it has since declined to about 270. The lack of traditional date gardens has meant that it has been possible to concentrate attention on vegetable production. The government has adopted a policy aimed at achieving a balance of food imports and exports, but there is undoubtedly a problem of declining quantity and quality of water resources.

484 The developing agriculture of the Middle East: opportunities and prospects.

R. M. Burrell, S. Hoyle, K. McLachlan, C. Parker. London: Graham & Trotman, 1976. 74p.

The fourth chapter, which is on Saudi Arabia, includes a map of agricultural developments on which Qatar is illustrated.

485 Fisheries of the Arabian peninsula.

William J. Donaldson. In: *Change and development in the Middle East: essays in honour of W. B. Fisher.* Edited by John I. Clarke, Howard Bowen-Jones. London, New York: Methuen, 1981, p. 189-98.

Qatar is mentioned a number of times in this survey of Arabian fisheries. The establishment of the shrimp fishing industry in the 1960s, with its labour coming mainly from the northern states of the UAE and from the Sultanate of Oman, followed by subsequent financial difficulties in the late 1970s is noted.

486 Agricultural development in a petroleum-based economy: Qatar.

M. F. Hassan. *Economic Development and Cultural Change*, vol. 27, no. 1 (1978), p. 145-67.

This paper evaluates Qatar's economy; the constraints on agricultural development in the form of adverse climatic conditions, land resources, soil conditions, water and irrigation; and Qatar's policy for agricultural developments in terms of its

495 The future of Gulf ports.
Anne M. Hughes. *Geography*, vol. 64, no. 1 (1979), p. 54-56.
Doha port, with 4.2 per cent of the trade of the Gulf area, is seen as being one of the most vulnerable in the region in the face of a possible decline in trade.

496 *Lloyds List* special report: Qatar.
Lloyds List, 1 Dec. 1978, p. 5-11.
Provides information on Qatar's use of oil revenues and trade, the Qatar Monetary Agency, and in particular details of the expansion of Doha port, Umm Said's industrial import-export port, and Qatar's partnership in Gulf Air.

497 Transportation in eastern Arabia.
Alexander Melamid. *Geographical Review*, vol. 52, no. 1 (1962), p. 122-24.
A brief report on the state of road transport in the region in the 1950s, which argues that modern transportation has brought about the end of local wars. Air flights from Ad Dawhah (Doha) in Qatar are mentioned.

498 Present trends show urgency of Pan-Arab action on ports.
Middle East, vol. 46 (1978), p. 72-73.
Notes Qatar's 27 million dollar port extension in an article on the lack of co-ordinated planning in the Gulf.

499 The Persian Gulf dhows: new notes on the classification of mid-Eastern sea-craft.
A. M. J. Prins. *Persica*, vol. 6 (1972-74), p. 157-78.
Although it does not specifically mention Qatar, this is a useful discussion of the types of boat used in the Gulf, and of its ports.

500 Ship repairing in Arabian Gulf ports.
Shipping World and Shipbuilder, no. 3929, vol. 170 (1977), p. 71, 73.
Notes that Bahrein Shipway Company Ltd. cleaned and painted royal yachts from Qatar in 1977.

501 Shipping in the Middle East.
Middle East Economic Digest, vol. 15, no. 7 (1971), special report. 8p.
This mentions the planned expansion of Qatar's ports.

502 **Civil aviation in the Gulf: the role of commercial interests in the issue of traffic rights.**
Elda I. Stifani. *Arabian Studies*, vol. 3 (1976), p. 29-50.
This paper includes details of Gulf Air, which is jointly owned by Bahrain, Qatar, the UAE and Oman. There are several mentions of Doha airport in connection with the civil aviation companies that utilize its facilities.

503 **Seaports and development in the Persian Gulf.**
Antony Raymond Walker. PhD thesis, University of Durham, Durham, England, 1981 (unpublished). 369p. 22 maps. bibliog.
Although mainly concerned with Kuwait, Bahrain and Dubai, this volume provides much interesting information on the ports of Doha and Umm Said, and the planned port of Jazirat Alyah in Qatar. It measures the extent of the existing dhow trading network, comments on the inter-relationship between port expansion projects and the pattern of economic development in the Gulf, and highlights problems relating to the overtonnaging of shipping services and port congestion in the Gulf.

504 **Port congestion: waiting times fall as port authorities try rough tactics.**
John Whelan. *Middle East Economic Digest*, vol. 21, no. 8 (25 Feb. 1977), p. 3-4.
This notes that the waiting time at Doha port in February 1977 was forty to forty-two days.

Employment and Manpower

505 The labour market performance in some Arab Gulf states.
Henry T. Azzam. In: *Issues in development: the Arab Gulf states.* Edited by May Ziwar Daftari. London: MD Research and Services, 1980, p. 27-45.

The author argues that the Arab Gulf states have a number of shared labour characteristics, particularly related to the fact that they have small and unskilled national workforces and therefore must rely increasingly on migrant workers. This has led to a dual labour market. Qatar has the smallest labour force in the Gulf, and also has the lowest percentage of females within the workforce. Umm Said is mentioned as an example of an enclave industrial development.

506 Arab manpower: the crisis of development.
John Stace Birks, Clive A. Sinclair. London: Croom Helm, 1980. 391p. map. bibliog.

Oil is seen as being a factor leading to great variations in the Arab world. Chapter 3 is devoted to Qatar, which is classified as a capital-rich state. Although immigrants account for more than half of the population they are not yet seen as a problem, since they are not politically articulate. The authors consider that the crisis facing Qatar is social, rather than economic, in that her society will become increasingly segmented and demarcated between national and non-national.

507 Economic and social implications of current development in the Arab Gulf: the oriental connection.
John Stace Birks, Clive A. Sinclair. In: *Social and economic development in the Arab Gulf.* Edited by Tim Niblock. London: Croom Helm, 1980, p. 135-60.

A study of the reasons behind, and consequences of, labour immigration into the Gulf states. It notes the increasing numbers of Asian labourers in Qatar and the

Employment and Manpower

development of enclave industrial areas, and concludes by depicting two scenarios for the labour market in the Gulf in 1985.

508 **International migration and development in the Arab region.**
John Stace Birks, Clive A. Sinclair. Geneva: International Labour Office, 1980. 175p. bibliog.
An analysis of labour migration in the Middle East, including thirty-eight pages of tables. Qatar, a country of major immigration resulting from the exploitation of oil, is discussed on p. 69-71. In 1970 one-third of Qatar's migrant labour was Iranian. In both 1970 and 1975 migrants comprised over four-fifths of the total labour force.

509 **International Migration Project country case study: the State of Qatar.**
John Stace Birks, Clive A. Sinclair. Durham, England: University of Durham, Department of Economics, 1978. 31p.
A study of the supply of, and demand for, labour in Qatar in the 1970s. It concludes that in the future many more migrant workers will travel to Qatar, mainly from Asia or the Far East, and that further expansion of the civil service will be necessary to handle the state's planned economic and social development.

510 **The nature and process of labour importing: the Arabian Gulf states of Kuwait, Bahrain, Qatar and the United Arab Emirates.**
John Stace Birks, Clive A. Sinclair. Geneva: International Labour Office, 1978. 87p. bibliog. (ILO World Employment Programme Research Working Paper, WEP 2-26/WP30).
Provides information on the supply of labour, economic development, labour demand, labour market, and present migration patterns in Qatar.

511 **Some aspects of the labour market in the Middle East, with special reference to the Gulf states.**
John Stace Birks, Clive A. Sinclair. *Journal of Developing Areas*, vol. 13, no. 3 (1979), p. 301-18.
An investigation into the manpower shortages and consequent high levels of expatriate labour to be found in the capital-rich Arab states. It estimates that 58.8 per cent of the population of Qatar in 1975 consisted of non-nationals, and that 81.1 per cent of the labour force was non-national. A crisis is forecast when the traditional labour supplies of these countries run dry.

512 **Manpower and employment problems in Kuwait and Qatar.**
May Ziwar Daftari. *Journal of the Gulf and Arabian Peninsula Studies*, vol. 6, no. 23 (1980), p. 67-108. (In Arabic with English summary).
Eighty per cent of the total labour force in Qatar is expatriate, and this paper argues that a potential does exist for increasing the pool of local labour by further investment in education planning, encouraging female employment, and

118

correcting locals' attitudes to manual labour. Sixty per cent of Qatar's employment is in the tertiary sector.

513 Migration and labour force in the oil-producing states of the Middle East.
F. Halliday. *Development and Change*, vol. 8, no. 3 (1977), p. 263-91.

A study of the changes in the composition of the oil-producing countries' labour forces which have been brought about as a result of increased oil revenues. Qatar is identified as a city state, where oil plays a fundamental role in foreign exchange earnings and where its impact is seen as consolidating the position of the ruling régime. Immigrants now form the majority of the population, and over three-quarters of the labour force.

514 The modernization of labor and labor law in the Arab Gulf states.
Enid Hill. Cairo: American University in Cairo, 1979. 113p. 2 maps. bibliog. (Cairo Papers in Social Science, monograph 2).

This paper explores the anomaly by which the creation of labour law has generally preceded the modernization of the legal systems in the Gulf. Qatar is seen as consisting almost entirely of urban dwellers, and it is stated that there is virtually no economic activity not directly related to the capitalist structure. It notes that the labour law of Qatar provides that workers should present their complaints to their employer in writing, and that the employer must reply within six days in writing. Copies of both letters must be sent to the Director of Labour. The Qatari Labour Court has jurisdiction over all disputes brought to it under the labour law. It also notes that committees of workers, known as *lajnat 'ummal*, have been formed in Qatar.

515 Education and manpower in the Arabian Gulf.
Robert Anton Mertz. Washington, DC: American Friends of the Middle East, 1972. 226p.

Qatar is discussed on p. 113-36 of this description and analysis of education and manpower needs in the Gulf. Details are provided of Qatar's population, economic position, educational framework, and labour force. The problems of having a large immigrant labour force are highlighted.

516 Labor markets and citizenship in Bahrayn and Qatar.
Emile A. Nakhleh. *Middle East Journal*, vol. 31, no. 2 (1977), p. 143-56.

This paper highlights the lack of an adequately trained indigenous labour force in Bahrayn and Qatar, which thus gives rise to a need to import thousands of foreign workers. It argues that, in contrast to Bahrayn, Qatar's labour tradition is barely a decade old, yet both governments view labour unrest as inimical to the national interest. Details of Qatar's labour law of 1962 are provided on p. 149, and of its citizenship law on p. 150-51.

Employment and Manpower

517 **Migration and employment in the Arab world: construction as a key policy variable.**
R. Paul Shaw. *International Labour Review*, vol. 118, no. 5 (1979), p. 589-605.

This paper, which mainly considers the effects of migration in OAPEC countries, emphasizes the severe data limitations inherent in such an investigation. In Qatar in 1970 16.9 per cent of the non-agricultural labour force was employed in construction, a lower figure than was to be found in most labour-importing countries of the Middle East, but non-nationals comprised 97.3 per cent of all construction workers, which was the highest figure for those countries investigated in the study.

L'immigration dans la péninsule arabique. (Immigration in the Arabian peninsula.)
See item no. 226.

Middle East economies in the 1970s: a comparative approach.
See item no. 347.

Persian Gulf studies.
See item no. 369.

Impact of technical change on the structure of the labour force in the ECWA region.
See item no. 529.

Statistics

518 **An economic survey of Qatar 1969-1973.**
Ahmed Abdou Ahmed. Doha: State of Qatar, Ministry of
Economy and Commerce, 1974. 106p.

Provides statistics on Qatar's agriculture, oil, production, commerce, industry,
foreign trade, insurance, prices, money and banking, government budgetary capital expenditure, and education.

519 **Demographic Yearbook.**
New York: United Nations, 1948- . annual.

A comprehensive collection of international demographic statistics prepared by the
UN covering 220 countries including Qatar.

520 **Economic survey of Qatar. Years 1976 and 1977.**
Doha: State of Qatar, Ministry of Economy and Commerce,
1978. 193p.

Provides comprehensive statistics on Qatar's oil, production, commercial and
industrial activity, foreign trade, agriculture, insurance, currency and banks, capital expenditure, balance of payments, prices, social services, communications and
transport, and public health.

521 **U.N. Statistical Yearbook.**
New York: United Nations, 1948- . annual.

Provides up-to-date summary economic and social statistics for many countries of
the world, including Qatar, for which details are available on population, fishing,
petroleum, energy production and consumption, trade, transport, and communications.

The Middle East: a handbook.
See item no. 1.

The Middle East and North Africa.
See item no. 25.

121

Statistics

Qatar Year Book 1978-79.
See item no. 41.

Bahrain, Qatar, and the United Arab Emirates: colonial past, present problems, and future prospects.
See item no. 287.

Qatar: MEED special report.
See item no. 374.

Education

522 **Educational development aspiration and implementation.**
Qatar: State of Qatar, Ministry of Education and Youth
Welfare, 1973. 116p.
A government publication showing in words and pictures the activities of the
Ministry of Education and Youth Welfare in the fields of education and culture
during the two years following independence.

523 **The development of education in Qatar, 1950-1977 with an
analysis of some educational problems.**
Abdulla Juma al-Kobaisi. PhD thesis, University of
Durham, Durham, England, 1979 (unpublished). 316p.
bibliog.
Since 1954 education in Qatar has expanded dramatically. This thesis describes
the traditional *kuttab* system of education based on the mosques, and provides a
complete analysis of the development of the new system, covering details of
curriculums, teachers and pupils, and concludes with suggestions and recommendations concerning educational quality.

524 **Islam and women: some experiments in Qatar.**
H. Malik. *Journal of South Asian and Middle Eastern
Studies*, vol. 4, no. 2 (1980), p. 3-9.
This study pays particular attention to the education of women in Qatar at
university level.

525 **Education in Kuwait, Bahrain and Qatar: an economic
assessment.**
C. A. Sinclair. PhD thesis, University of Durham,
Durham, England, 1977 (unpublished). 383p. bibliog.
This study uses 'rate-of-return' analysis and 'manpower assessment' to examine
the effects of education on economic development in three countries of the Gulf.
The demographic development of Qatar is discussed in chapter 3, the relations

between its economic development and the labour market in chapter 4, and the development of human resources in Qatar in chapter 6.

526 **Education in the Arab states in the light of the Abu Dhabi conference 1977.**
Abdelhadi Tazi.   Unesco, 1980. 81p.
This booklet is based on the working documents and final reports for the 1977 conference on education in the Arab states. It includes numerous tables of educational data for the countries of the region including Qatar.

The United Arab Emirates: a modern history.
See item no. 157.

Education and manpower in the Arabian Gulf.
See item no. 515.

Qatar celebrates 10 years of independence.
See item no. 535.

Science and Technology

527 **Arab telecommunications: *Financial Times* survey.**
Financial Times, 6 Jan. 1981, p. 9-12.
Total spending on telecommunications in Qatar over the period 1977-81 is estimated at 65 million dollars. Within this report on telecommunications throughout the Arab world there are brief details of the new digital-based national telephone exchange to be introduced in Qatar in 1982.

528 **Science and technology in the development of the Arab states.**
Paris: Unesco, 1977. 327p. (Science Policy Studies and Documents, no. 41).
The final report and working document of the Conference of Ministers of Arab States Responsible for the Application of Science and Technology to Development (CASTARAB), held at Rabat in August 1976, in which Qatar took part. It provides information on current practices and policies of Arab states in the field of science and technology.

529 **Impact of technical change on the structure of the labour force in the ECWA region.**
Nadja M. El-Shishini. In: *Technology transfer and change in the Arab world.* Edited by A. B. Zahlan. Oxford, England; New York: Pergamon Press, 1978, p. 205-21.
Details of Qatar's population and labour force are given in this paper, which evaluates how technology has changed the labour composition of the region.

530 **Telecommunications in the Arab world: a special report.**
The Times (UK), 2 Feb. 1981, p. 17-19.
This report on telecommunications notes that in Qatar the number of telephones to each individual subscriber is as high as twenty.

Science and Technology

531 **The status of science and technology in the Western Asian region.**
United Nations Economic Commission for Western Asia, NRST Division, presented by R. Van der Graaf. In: *Technology transfer and change in the Arab world.* Edited by A. B. Zahlan. Oxford, England; New York: Pergamon Press, 1978, p. 51-94.
This paper includes details of Qatar's imports and industrial research and development.

532 **Technology transfer and change in the Arab world: a seminar of the United Nations Economic Commission for Western Asia.**
Edited by A. B. Zahlan. Oxford, England; New York: Pergamon Press, 1978. 506p.
The papers by Van der Graaf, El-Shishini, and Zureik include specific mentions of Qatar's labour force.

533 **Values, social organization and technology change in the Arab world.**
Elia T. Zureik. In: *Technology transfer and change in the Arab world.* Edited by A. B. Zahlan. Oxford, England; New York: Pergamon Press, 1978, p. 185-203.
This paper notes details of Qatar's gross national product in 1973, and observes that 90.3 per cent of the total stock of scientists and engineers in Qatar in 1974 were non-national.

126

The Arts

534 **The poetic spirit in Qatar's history.**
Darwish Mostafa Al-Far. *Weekly Gulf Times*, 21 May
1981.
A brief account of Qatar's past and present poets. It discusses Tarfah ibn al-Abd, al-Mothaqqab al-Abdi, ibn al-Fuja'ah and the ruler-poet Sheikh Qassim ibn Mohammed al-Thani.

535 **Qatar celebrates 10 years of independence.**
International Herald Tribune, 2 Sept. 1981, p. 5.
An information message prepared by Qatar's Ministry of Information covering the advances made in education, industrial development, and culture in the form of the National Theatre and Museum.

536 **The old Amiri Palace Doha, Qatar.**
G. R. H. Wright. Doha: Qatar National Museum, 1975.
39p. 2 maps.
A description of the old palace at Doha, including detailed plans and architectural drawings, and a brief account of the restoration work undertaken.

The Persian Gulf states.
See item no. 9.

127

Sports and
Recreation

537 **Falconry in Arabia.**
Mark Allen.   London: Orbis Publishing, 1980. 143p. 2
maps. bibliog.
Qatar is but briefly mentioned in this essential text for anyone interested in
falconry in Arabia, which covers the subject from the methods of the past to
those of today using air-conditioned cars. Qatar is one of the regions along the
shores of the Gulf where hawks are traditionally trapped, and the author also
notes that the repeated outbreaks of disease in a captive herd of oryx in Qatar
indicate that these magnificent beasts are mortally averse to crowding.

538 **Qatar: a special presentation by the state of Qatar to mark
the staging in its capital, Doha, of the fourth Gulf football
tournament.**
Time, 28 July 1976, p. C1-C8.
In addition to a report on the fourth Gulf football tournament this includes brief
details of Qatar's politics, economy, public services, and infrastructure.

539 **Leisure, recreational and sporting facilities in the Arab states
of the Gulf.**
Philip Stephens.   London: London Chamber of Commerce
and Industry, 1977. 33p.
This report aims to provide information on the expansion of leisure and
recreational facilities in the Gulf for British architects, consultants, and suppliers.
It notes that the pace of leisure development in Qatar is slower than in other
Gulf states, but that football is a very popular sport.

128

Mass Media

540 **Al-Ahad.** (Sunday.)
Doha: Khalifa Abdulla al-Hussaini. weekly.
An Arabic magazine.

541 **Almurjan.** (Coral.)
Doha: Gulf Hotels Group, Feb. 1976- . quarterly.
An English magazine about the localities in which Gulf Hotels operate, providing information on cultural, economic and historical features. It also contains a general section on information about Bahrain, Oman and Qatar.

542 **Al-Arab.** (The Arab.)
Doha: Arabian Newspaper Publishing and Printing House, 5 Feb. 1970- . daily.
An Arabic newspaper, the first to be published in Qatar, covering daily events within the Gulf region and the remainder of the world. Circulation 15,000.

543 **Arrayah.** (The Banner.)
Doha: Gulf Publishing and Printing Organization, 10 May 1979- . weekly; 27 January 1980- . daily.
A new Arabic newspaper, the sister paper of the *Gulf Times*. It includes comments on local and international events, and contains occasional special reports on aspects of the country such as health and agriculture. The daily edition commenced publication on 27 January 1980.

544 **Al-Dawri.** (The League.)
Doha: Sheikh Rashid bin Waidah al-Thani. weekly.
An Arabic sports newspaper.

Mass Media

545 **Diaruna wal Alam.** (Our Country and the World.)
Doha: Ministry of Finance and Petroleum. monthly.
An economic review paying particular attention to petroleum. It is half in English and half in Arabic.

546 **Al-Doha.** (Doha.)
Doha: Ministry of Information, 1 Jan. 1976- . monthly.
An Arabic magazine on cultural and economic aspects of Qatar.

547 **Al-Fajr.** (The Dawn.)
Doha: Qatar National Printing Press. weekly.
An Arabic newspaper.

548 **The Gulf Times.**
Doha: Gulf Publishing and Printing Organization, 10 Dec.
1978- . weekly; 22 January 1981- . daily.
The main English newspaper printed in Qatar and circulated throughout the Gulf. Both the weekly and the daily contain financial, economic and political news relating to the whole world, and have a sports coverage which includes European events. The weekly has a cartoon supplement and includes diverse features on Qatar. The daily edition commenced publication on 22 January 1981 and has a circulation of 6,000, the weekly of 10,000.

549 **Al-Jawhara.** (The Jewel.)
Doha: Khalifa Abdulla al-Hussaini. monthly.
An Arabic women's magazine.

550 **Al-Khalij al-Jadeed.** (The New Gulf.)
Doha: Ministry of Information, 1 March 1976- . monthly.
An Arabic magazine giving details on the Gulf's cultural heritage and recent economic changes.

551 **Al-Mishal.** (The Torch.)
Doha: Qatar Petroleum Producing Authority. monthly.
A magazine covering petroleum developments in the country.

552 **Al-Ouroba.** (Arabism.)
Doha: Arabian Newspaper Printing and Publishing House, 5
March 1972- . weekly.
A general Arabic magazine of events and news, the sister paper of *Al-Arab*, and the first Qatar weekly. Circulation 12,000.

553 **The Arab press: news media and political process in the Arab world.**
William A. Rugh. Syracuse, New York: Syracuse University Press, 1979. 205p.
Provides details of media statistics, newspapers, radio and television, and the position of foreign journalists in Qatar.

554 **Al-Saqr.** (The Hawk.)
Doha: Military Sports Association, 1 March 1977- . weekly.
A sports magazine, mainly concentrating on military teams and sporting events, but with some international coverage. Prior to January 1982 it appeared monthly.

555 **Al-Tarbiya.** (Education.)
Doha: Ministry of Education. bimonthly.
A ministry publication on recent educational changes and developments.

556 **Al-Umma.** (The Nation.)
Doha: Sharia Courts and Religious Affairs, Nov. 1980- . monthly.
A publication covering religious affairs in Qatar.

Bibliographies

557 **The states of the Arabian peninsula and Gulf littoral: a selected bibliography.**
John Duke Anthony.   Washington, DC: Middle East Institute, 1973. 21p.

A partially annotated bibliography concentrating on the governmental systems, political dynamics, international relations and economies of the Arabian peninsula and Gulf states.

558 **Arab culture and society in change: a partially annotated bibliography of books and articles in English, French, German and Italian.**
Compiled by the staff of the Centre d'Etudes pour le Monde Arabe Moderne.   Beirut: Dar el-Mashreq, 1973. 318p.

The main theme of this bibliography is the encounter between traditional values of Arab consciousness and the new values of Western culture. It is concerned with the period 1914-73. It includes author, persons, regions and selected subjects indexes.

559 **Saudi Arabia.**
Frank A. Clements. Oxford, England: Clio Press; Santa Barbara, California: American Bibliographical Center-Clio Press, 1979. 197p. map.

An annotated bibliography which includes many references on Arabia in general, and one (342) on Qatar in particular.

560 **Le Golfe persique: introduction bibliographique.** (The Persian
Gulf: bibliographical introduction.)
Mohammad-Reza Djalili.   Geneva: Centre Asiatique,
Institut Universitaire de Hautes Etudes Internationales,
1979. 92p.
This bibliography is divided into three parts: the first covers general works, the
second individual countries, and the third the major problems facing the Gulf.
Qatar is detailed specifically on p. 45-46.

561 **Ports of the Arabian peninsula: a guide to the literature.**
H. Dodgeon, A. M. Findlay.   Durham, England: Centre for
Middle Eastern and Islamic Studies, Durham University,
1979. 49p. (Occasional Papers Series, no. 7).
An introductory bibliography to the ports of the Gulf, mentioning Doha and
Umm Said in Qatar.

562 **A bibliography of articles on the Middle East, 1959-1967.**
Compiled by Uri Dotan, edited by Avigdor Levy.   Tel Aviv:
Mif'al Hashichpul, 1970. 227p. (Shiloah Center's Teaching
and Research Aids).
A bibliography on the Middle East, mainly of articles in periodicals in Israeli
libraries. Author index only.

563 **Saudi Arabia and the Gulf states.**
Wendy Fiander.   London: Statistics and Market Intelligence
Library, 1979. rev. ed. 48p. (Sources of Statistics and
Market Information, 7, revised).
This useful publication provides an annotated bibliography of the background,
business conditions, directories and statistics of Bahrain, Kuwait, Qatar, Saudi
Arabia and the UAE. Qatar is specifically referred to in references 50-57, 114-
36, and 164-66.

564 **Bibliography on south western Asia.**
Henry Field.   Coral Gables, Florida: University of Miami
Press, 1953-62. 7 vols.
An anthropogeographical and natural history bibliography of the area from the
Nile to the Indus, and from Anatolia and the Caucasus to the Arabian Sea.
Author index only.

565 **Analytical guide to the bibliographies on the Arabian
peninsula.**
G. L. Geddes.   Denver, Colorado: American Institute of
Islamic Studies, 1974. 50p.
A list of seventy bibliographies on the Arabian peninsula, the Gulf and the Red
Sea, together with annotations concerning content and arrangement. Qatar is
mentioned in numbers 59 and 60.

Bibliographies

566 **Bibliography of the Arabian peninsula.**
Harry W. Hazard, Robert W. Crawford (and others). New
Haven, Connecticut: Human Relations Area Files, 1956.
256p.
A list of articles and books compiled for the American Geographical Society on
the subject of Arabia. No index.

567 **Middle East and Islam: a bibliographical introduction.**
Edited by Derek Hopwood, Diana Grimwood Jones. Zug,
Switzerland: Inter Documentation Company, 1972. 368p.
A broad introduction to the Middle East. Qatar is generally included in sections
on Arabia. Author index only.

568 **Source book on the Arabian Gulf states: Arabian Gulf in
general, Kuwait, Bahrain, Qatar, and Oman.**
Soraya M. Kabeel. Kuwait: Kuwait University Press, 1975.
427p.
The book is divided into three parts: an introductory survey providing economic,
historical and geographical information on each country; a bibliographical survey;
and a general index. Qatar is discussed on p. 34-37, and within each section of
the bibliography. It provides a useful introduction to the region.

569 **Bibliography of the Arabian peninsula.**
Eric Macro. Coral Gables, Florida: University of Miami
Press, 1958. 80p.
A bibliography compiled mainly between 1945-50. Author index only.

570 **A guide to manuscripts and documents in the British Isles
relating to the Middle East and North Africa.**
Compiled by Noel Matthews, M. Doreen Wainwright, edited
by J. D. Pearson. Oxford, England: Oxford University
Press, 1980. 482p.
The references to Qatar in this volume are found mainly in the list of India
Office records.

571 **Middle East Journal.**
Washington, DC: Middle East Institute, 1947- . quarterly.
Each issue contains a bibliographical section organized by subject and geographi-
cal area.

572 **Index Islamicus.**
J. D. Pearson. Cambridge, England: W. Heffer & Sons,
1958 (1906-55), 1962 (supplement 1956-60), 1967
(supplement 1961-65). London: Mansell, 1972 (supplement
1966-70), 1977 (supplement 1971-75).
A catalogue of articles on Islamic subjects in periodicals and other collective
publications.

573 **The Quarterly Index Islamicus: Current Books, Articles and
Papers on Islamic Studies.**
Edited by J. D. Pearson. London: Mansell, Jan. 1977- .
quarterly.
Lists articles from a wide range of periodicals arranged by country.

574 **The Arabian peninsula: a selected, annotated list of
periodicals, books and articles in English.**
Prepared under the direction of the US Library of Congress
Near East Section, Division of Orientalia. Washington,
DC: US Government Printing Office, 1951. Reprinted, New
York: Greenwood Press, 1969. 111p.
Emphasis in this bibliography is placed on the geography, ethnology, economy
and politics of Arabia. Author index only.

The Arabian peninsula and annotated bibliography.
See item no. 236.

Index

The index is a single alphabetical sequence of authors (personal and corporate), titles of publications and subjects. Index entries refer both to the main items and to other works mentioned in the notes to each item. Title entries are in italics. Numeration refers to the items as numbered.

A

'Abbasid era 210
Abd, Tarfah Ibn al- 534
Abdallah bin Qasim al-Thani, Shaikh 220
Abdallah, Muhammad ibn 174
Abdi, al-Mothaqqab al- 534
'Abdul Rahman, Imam 206
Abdullah, Muhammad Morsy 157
ABECOR country report: Qatar 5
Abelson, D. S. 2
Abir, M. 243, 308, 343
Abu Dhabi
  relations with Qatar 157, 221, 245, 288, 320−321, 457
  relations with Qatar, 19th century 203
Abu Hakima, A. M. 158, 244, 268
Abu Haydar, G. 241
Abu Haydar, N. 241
Abu Nab, I. 159
Adams, M. 1, 17
Adler, J. 436
Administration 18, 22, 26, 38−40, 294−295, 359, 420
  British period 300

Admiralty, Naval Intelligence Division, Great Britain 14
Admiralty War Staff, Intelligence Division, Great Britain 15
Aerial photography 81
Africano, L. 344
Agency law 306
Agricultural development 479, 490
  maps 484
  role of oil 486
Agriculture 6, 8−9, 18, 20, 26, 28, 30, 32−35, 47, 74, 242, 347, 357, 360, 363, 374, 378−380, 396, 402, 419, 428−429, 483, 486, 490
  influence of nomads 489
  labour 486
  livestock 487
  maps 64
  statistics 518, 520
  tenant farms 482
  water resources 479, 482−483, 488−489
Agwani, M. S. 245
Ahad, Al- 540
Ahmad bin Ali al-Thani, Shaikh 21, 166, 197, 249
Ahmad bin Khalifa, Shaikh 162
Ahmad bin Muhammad al-Thani 206

137

143

145

Key, K. K. 360
Khalid, Bani 249
Khalifa, A. M. 274
Khalifa, Al-, family 231, 244
 relations with Qatar 187—188
Khalifa bin Hamad al-Thani,
 Shaikh 21, 30, 159, 197, 249,
 314, 319, 411
Khalifa, Shaikh Ahmad bin 162
Khalifa, Shaikh Muhammad bin 189
Khalij al-Jadeed, Al- 550
Khan, M. S. Saleem 275
Khawr 95
Khawr al-'Udaid 173, 320
 boundary dispute 157, 288, 321
 geology 92
Khawr Hassan 212
Khomeini régime, Iran 246
Khudr, A. S. 425
Kilner, P. 20
Kings of Harmuz 116
Kings of Persia 116
*Kitāb al-fawā'id fī uṣūl al-baḥr wa
 'l-qawā'id* 213
Knapp, V. 296
Kniphausen, Tido von 175
Kobaisi, A. J. al- 523
Koninklijke 106
Kumar, R. 190—191
Kutschera, C. 21
Kuwait and her neighbours 231
*Kuwait, Bahrain, Qatar, Oman,
 Arabemiraten. En guide för
 affarsmän och turister* 23
Kuwari, A. Khalifa al- 361

L

Labour 26, 35, 347, 355, 382, 402,
 420, 425, 505, 509—511, 515
 1963 strike 289, 336
 agricultural 486
 construction industry 517
 engineers 533
 immigrant 187, 226, 270, 285, 347,
  369—370, 425, 485, 505—513,
  515—517, 533, 539
 impact of technology 529, 532
 Labour Court 514
 law 348, 514, 516
 role in economic development 525
 scientists 533

women 505, 512
worker committees 514
Lackner, H. 276
Land 486, 490
 prices 435
Land use 63, 73
Landen, R. G. 192
Langella, V. 277
Language 9, 230
Lannois, P. 22
Laqueur, W. 322—323
Larsen, C. E. 57
Law 39, 297, 305
 agency 306
 British jurisdiction 301
 commercial 297, 420
 Islamic 297
 labour 348, 514, 516
 maritime 298, 302—303, 367
 nationality 227, 516
 offshore boundaries 298, 302—303
 oil concessions 307
 oil industry 367, 468—469
 sharia 297
Lawless, R. I. 224
Leatherdale, J. 81
Ledger, D. 278
Lees, G. M. 82—83, 461
*Legal development in Arabia. A
 selection of articles and addresses
 on the Arabian Gulf* 297
*Legal framework for oil concessions in
 the Arab world* 307
*Legal status of the Arabian Gulf
 states: a study of their treaty
 relations and their international
 problems* 295
Legal system 192, 294—297
 courts 242
 Labour Court 514
Leisure 32, 539
*Leisure, recreational and sporting
 facilities in the Arab states of the
 Gulf* 539
Levy, A. 562
Liebesny, H. J. 300—302, 324
Life and customs 13, 22, 24, 28, 39,
 42, 418, 420
 bedouin 10, 30—31, 34
 visiting 237

150

151

O

162

Map of Qatar

This map shows the more important towns and other features.

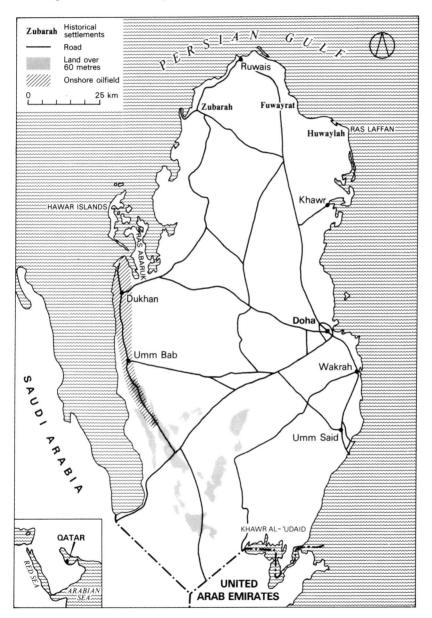

Legend:
- **Zubarah** — Historical settlements
- —— Road
- Land over 60 metres
- Onshore oilfield
- 0 — 25 km

PERSIAN GULF

Ruwais
Zubarah   Fuwayrat
Huwaylah   RAS LAFFAN
Khawr
HAWAR ISLANDS
RAS ABARUK
Dukhan
Doha
Umm Bab
Wakrah
Umm Said
SAUDI ARABIA
KHAWR AL-'UDAID
UNITED ARAB EMIRATES

QATAR
RED SEA
ARABIAN SEA